THE IRISH AMERICANS

THE IRISH AMERICANS

J. F. Watts

CHELSEA HOUSE PUBLISHERS

New York   Philadelphia

Cover Photograph: Prominent Irish Americans review New York City's Police Parade in 1908.

Editor-in-Chief: Nancy Toff
Executive Editor: Remmel T. Nunn
Managing Editor: Karyn Gullen Browne
Copy Chief: Juliann Barbato
Picture Editor: Adrian G. Allen
Art Director: Giannella Garrett
Manufacturing Manager: Gerald Levine

Staff for THE IRISH AMERICANS:

Senior Editor: Sam Tanenhaus
Text Editor: Constance Jones
Assistant Editor: Abigail Meisel
Editorial Assistant: Karen Schimmel
Copyeditors: Michael Goodman, Terrance Dolan
Senior Designer: Laurie Jewell
Designer: Noreen M. Lamb
Production Coordinator: Laura McCormick
Cover Illustration: Paul Biniasz
Banner Design: Hrana L. Janto

Creative Director: Harold Steinberg

3 5 7 9 8 6 4

Library of Congress Cataloging in Publication Data

Watts, J. F. (Jim F.), 1935–
    The Irish Americans

    (The Peoples of North America)
    Bibliography: p.
    Includes index.
    Summary: Discusses the history, culture, and religion of the Irish, factors encouraging their emigration, and their acceptance as an ethnic group in North America.
    1. Irish Americans—Juvenile literature.
[1. Irish Americans] I. Title. II. Series.
E184.I6W33 1988   973'.049162   87-15787
ISBN 0-87754-855-2
        0-7910-0267-5 (pbk.)

CONTENTS

A
NATION
OF
NATIONS

Daniel Patrick Moynihan

The Constitution of the United States begins: "We the People of the United States . . ." Yet, as we know, the United States is not made up of a single group of people. It is made up of many peoples. Immigrants from Europe, Asia, Africa, and Central and South America settled in North America seeking a new life filled with opportunities unavailable in their homeland. Coming from many nations, they forged one nation and made it their own. More than 100 years ago, Walt Whitman expressed this perception of America as a melting pot: "Here is not merely a nation, but a teeming Nation of nations."

Although the ingenuity and acts of courage of these immigrants, our ancestors, shaped the North American way of life, we sometimes take their contributions for granted. This fine series, *The Peoples of North America,* examines the experiences and contributions of the immigrants and how these contributions determined the future of the United States and Canada.

Immigrants did not abandon their ethnic traditions when they reached the shores of North America. Each ethnic group had its own customs and traditions, and each brought different experiences, accomplishments, skills, values, styles of dress, and tastes in food that lingered long after its arrival. Yet this profusion of differences created a singularity, or bond, among the immigrants.

The United States and Canada are unusual in this respect. Whereas religious and ethnic differences have sparked intolerance throughout the rest of the world—from the 17th-century religious wars to the 19th-century nationalist movements in Europe to the near extermination of the Jewish people under Nazi Germany—North Americans have struggled to learn how to respect each other's differences and live in harmony.

Millions of immigrants from scores of homelands brought diversity to our continent. In a mass migration, some 12 million immigrants passed through the waiting rooms of New York's Ellis Island; thousands more came to the West Coast. At first, these immigrants were welcomed because labor was needed to meet the demands of the Industrial Age. Soon, however, the new immigrants faced the prejudice of earlier immigrants who saw them as a burden on the economy. Legislation was passed to limit immigration. The Chinese Exclusion Act of 1882 was among the first laws closing the doors to the promise of America. The Japanese were also effectively excluded by this law. In 1924, Congress set immigration quotas on a country-by-country basis.

Such prejudices might have triggered war, as they did in Europe, but North Americans chose negotiation and compromise, instead. This determination to resolve differences peacefully has been the hallmark of the peoples of North America.

The remarkable ability of Americans to live together as one people was seriously threatened by the issue of slavery. It was a symptom of growing intolerance in the world. Thousands of settlers from the British Isles had arrived in the colonies as indentured servants, agreeing to work for a specified number of years on farms or as apprentices in return for passage to America and room and board. When the first Africans arrived in the then-British colonies during the 17th century, some colonists thought that they too should be treated as indentured servants. Eventually, the question of whether the Africans should be viewed as indentured, like the English, or as slaves who could be owned for life, was considered in a Maryland court. The court's calamitous decree held that blacks were slaves bound to lifelong servitude, and so were their children. America went through a time of moral examination and civil war before it finally freed African slaves and their descendants. The principle that all people are created equal had faced its greatest challenge and survived.

Yet the court ruling that set blacks apart from other races fanned flames of discrimination that burned long after slavery was abolished—and that still flicker today. The concept of racism had existed for centuries in countries throughout the world. For instance, when the Manchus conquered China in the 17th century, they decreed that Chinese and Manchus could not intermarry. To impress their superiority on the conquered Chinese, the Manchus ordered all Chinese men to wear their hair in a long braid called a queue.

By the 19th century, some intellectuals took up the banner of racism, citing Charles Darwin. Darwin's scientific studies hypothesized that highly evolved animals were dominant over other animals. Some advocates of this theory applied it to humans, asserting that certain races were more highly evolved than others and thus were superior.

This philosophy served as the basis for a new form of discrimination, not only against nonwhite people but also against various ethnic groups. Asians faced harsh discrimination and were depicted by popular 19th-century newspaper cartoonists as depraved, degenerate, and deficient in intelligence. When the Irish flooded American cities to escape the famine in Ireland, the cartoonists caricatured the typical "Paddy" (a common term for Irish immigrants) as an apelike creature with jutting jaw and sloping forehead.

By the 20th century, racism and ethnic prejudice had given rise to virulent theories of a Northern European master race. When Adolf Hitler came to power in Germany in 1933, he popularized the notion of Aryan supremacy. "Aryan," a term referring to the Indo-European races, was applied to so-called superior physical characteristics such as blond hair, blue eyes, and delicate facial features. Anyone with darker and heavier features was considered inferior. Buttressed by these theories, the German Nazi state from 1933 to 1945 set out to destroy European Jews, along with Poles, Russians, and other groups considered inferior. It nearly succeeded. Millions of these people were exterminated.

The tragedies brought on by ethnic and racial intolerance throughout the world demonstrate the importance of North America's efforts to create a society free of prejudice and inequality.

A relatively recent example of the New World's desire to resolve ethnic friction nonviolently is the solution the Canadians found to a conflict between two ethnic groups. A long-standing dispute as to whether Canadian culture was properly English or French resurfaced in the mid-1960s, dividing the peoples of the French-speaking Quebec Province from those of the English-speaking provinces. Relations grew tense, then bitter, then violent. The Royal Commission on Bilingualism and Biculturalism was established to study the growing crisis and to propose measures to ease the tensions. As a result of the commission's recommendations, all official documents and statements from the national government's capital at Ottawa are now issued in both French and English, and bilingual education is encouraged.

The year 1980 marked a coming of age for the United States's ethnic heritage. For the first time, the U.S. Census asked people about their ethnic background. Americans chose from more than 100 groups, including French Basque, Spanish Basque, French Canadian, Afro-American, Peruvian, Armenian, Chinese, and Japanese. The ethnic group with the largest response was English (49.6 million). More than 100 million Americans claimed ancestors from the British Isles, which includes England, Ireland, Wales, and Scotland. There were almost as many Germans (49.2 million) as English. The Irish-American population (40.2 million) was third, but the next largest ethnic group, the Afro-Americans, was a distant fourth (21 million). There was a sizable group of French ancestry (13 million), as well as of Italian (12 million). Poles, Dutch, Swedes, Norwegians, and Russians followed. These groups, and other smaller ones, represent the wondrous profusion of ethnic influences in North America.

Canada, too, has learned more about the diversity of its population. Studies conducted during the French/English conflict determined that Canadians were descended from Ukrainians, Germans, Italians, Chinese, Japanese, native Indians, and Eskimos, among others. Canada found it had no ethnic majority, although nearly half of its immigrant population had come from the British Isles. Canada, like the United States, is a land of immigrants for whom mutual tolerance is a matter of reason as well as principle.

The people of North America are the descendants of one of the greatest migrations in history. And that migration is not over. Koreans, Vietnamese, Nicaraguans, Cubans, and many others are heading for the shores of North America in large numbers. This mix of cultures shapes every aspect of our lives. To understand ourselves, we must know something about our diverse ethnic ancestry. Nothing so defines the North American nations as the motto on the Great Seal of the United States: *E Pluribus Unum*—Out of Many, One.

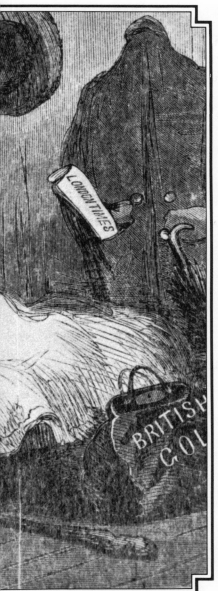

*"Politics makes strange bedfellows"
is the theme of this Civil war
cartoon, which accuses Irish
Americans of cozying up to English
capitalists to promote a "peace
platform" in the 1864 presidential
election.*

A
SUCCESS
STORY

The 40 million Americans who claim Irish descent belong to one of the largest and most successful ethnic groups in the United States. They inhabit every region of the nation and populate countless cities, suburbs, and rural communities. As an economic group they are equally dispersed; many are skilled laborers, others operate businesses, and, as of 1980, Irish Americans were more likely than their fellow citizens to be professionals and managers. Their collective role in politics and religion is enormous, and they have contributed mightily to commerce and the arts. Indeed Irish Americans have had so great an influence on our culture that it is almost impossible to think of them as an ethnic population.

Yet until quite recently Irish Americans were excluded from the social mainstream. The Irish immigrants who landed in this country in the 19th century often faced a New World version of the very obstacles that had stunted their lives in the Old World. In some places Irish Catholics were not allowed to vote or worship. Subsequent generations were stuck at the bottom of the social heap,

Tammany Hall, the New York City political "machine" dominated by Irish Americans, became notorious in the late 19th century.

working 12–hour days at menial jobs and living squalidly in overcrowded tenements.

Bleak as conditions in America were, however, they differed from those in Ireland in one essential way: The newness of the North American continent and the vitality of its institutions inspired the immigrants to better their lot. As their numbers increased, they used the democratic process to assert their political rights, especially in major cities; and the changing shape of our nation's ethnic makeup eventually enabled Irish Americans to clear a space in a culturally diverse landscape, offering their children the promise of a more rewarding future.

For all the remarkable gains this ethnic group has made, there is another side to their record of advancement and success, one scarcely imaginable even a generation ago. Irish Americans have begun to lose their distinctive ethnic identity. In 1928, when Alfred E. Smith was the Democratic nominee for the presidency of the United States, voters were acutely aware that he was Irish; the same was true in 1960, when John F. Kennedy became the first Irish-Catholic chief executive. But few people today know that the 40th president, Ronald Reagan, is a third-generation Irish American.

Reagan's Irish ancestry is generally overlooked because, to put it bluntly, he is not a Catholic, and the intense hostility often directed against Irish Americans has always been focused on Catholicism more than Irishness. The experience of the first Irish immigrants, perhaps more than that of any other ethnic group, reminds us of a startling fact: Until the late 19th century, the United States was almost exclusively a Protestant nation with little tolerance for other religions, even though many of

America's first settlers were themselves religious dissidents.

The United States began as a Protestant country, but it also evolved from a set of colonies chiefly inhabited by immigrants from the English speaking British Isles. Irish Americans were thus spared the task of learning a new tongue and had a head start on other 19th-century arrivals, most of whom came from Germany and Scandinavia.

The familiarity of North American culture also reinforced some unfortunate ancestral traits the group had acquired during long centuries of suffering in their homeland. As victims of a cruel sharecropping system, for example, many Irish developed an aversion to farming; subsequently the first immigrant generations spurned the vast agricultural resources of their adopted country and instead clustered in major port cities on the eastern seaboard, where job opportunities were limited and living conditions abominable.

This same pattern was repeated in Canada, where more than 500,000 Irish had immigrated by the 1850s. There too they usually congregated in port cities where they were exploited as a source of cheap labor. Even those who ventured into outlying areas shied away from tilling the soil. As a whole, the group fared so poorly that many Irish Canadians migrated again—to the United States, which had more cities, more employment, and fewer ties to Great Britain.

Great Britain had been a source of Irish resentment since the 12th century, when it invaded Ireland and inaugurated a tragic relationship between the countries that continues today. This rivalry influenced the attitudes of the first Irish Americans, many of whom equated the English-

American majority with those who had oppressed them in the old country. They were not entirely misguided in that belief. In the mid-19th century, America still bore the English stamp—not only in its language, but also in its distrust of the Roman Catholic church, its animosity toward alien cultures, and its ingrained class distinctions.

In response, Irish immigrants sometimes blundered into actions that recalled the violence and mob rule they occasionally resorted to in the Old World. Irish-American history includes a number of episodes that hardened other Americans against the Irish and reinforced stereotypes of Irish brutality and barbarism.

On the whole, though, Irish Americans willingly accepted the limits of the system in their efforts to improve it. Indeed, no other ethnic group has had such a profound impact on American democracy. Beginning in the cities, immigrants used the vote to assert their collective will, eventually gaining control of the Democratic party, an accomplishment whose reverberations reached the White House in 1960 with the close election of John F. Kennedy.

More importantly, Irish Americans introduced an ingredient so vital to American life that today we take it for granted—cultural diversity. The first Protestant colonists had a fixed idea of what sort of community ought to be established in the New World and of who deserved a place in it. Catholics, as a rule, did not fit their narrow criteria. It is perhaps the greatest achievement of the Irish Americans that they expanded that initial vision, adding to it an openness and generosity that now belong among the supreme virtues of the American character.

Irish-American policemen help improve the image of the group as a whole.

The Irish-American story has a happy outcome, but it begins sadly, even terribly, with the sufferings of a small nation, and proceeds through the hardships weathered by several immigrant generations. It is a story filled with acts of courage and cowardice, of anarchy and constructive reform. It is also a story of how prejudice acted as a spur to ethnic pride, and of how that pride in turn helped bring an end to prejudice.

In the end, the barriers erected to keep Irish Americans "in their place" strengthened family relationships so that they bridged generational divides, led persecuted Irish Catholics to gather in parishes where they proudly expressed their intense faith, and encouraged second-generation immigrants to unite against the dismal tenement life of the inner cities and to upgrade miserable conditions in the workplace.

The privileged position occupied by so many Irish Americans today is an ideal vantage point from which to survey the extraordinary distance traveled by the group in the 150 years since the first large wave of immigrants came to our shores. The closer we examine those pioneers—the first Irish Americans—the more familiar they seem: The qualities that enabled them to survive, and often to triumph, exist today as part of our common heritage, passed down to all of us, even those without a drop of Irish blood. ∾

England's Henry II invaded Ireland in 1152.

CATHOLICS AND CELTS

I reland is an island approximately the size of Maine, located directly west of Great Britain, a nation it has been feuding with since 1152. In that year Pope Adrian, the only English pope in Roman Catholic history, granted Ireland as a feudal property to Henry II, King of England, who promptly sent thousands of English colonists across the Irish Sea.

By the late 12th and early 13th centuries, English settlements covered two thirds of Ireland. The invaders built towns, churches, and manors, and established markets and fairs. In 1204 they erected Dublin Castle, which became the center of a government that included a parliament, a national tax office, a court system, sheriffs, and other institutions that transformed Ireland into a carbon copy of Great Britain.

This kind of foreign domination was not new to the Irish; in 1014 they had finally ousted the Vikings, who had invaded in 795 and who, like the British, had modernized the country. The Vikings built Ireland's first towns, including Dublin—still the country's greatest city—and introduced coinage and the ox-drawn plow. But in those times Ireland was not yet a unified country; it was instead a loose collection of kingships. By the time the English invaded, Ireland had a single monarch, a system of local rulers, and national laws. It was also tied to the European continent through a network of monasteries that were among the most advanced in the West, spreading Christian teachings to distant countries. Hence it was a severe indignity to be under the thumb of a nearby nation that was in many ways its inferior. Still the Irish coexisted with their conquerors until the 16th century, when a chain of events altered the course of Western history, and also the course of English-Irish relations.

The transformation began quietly enough in Germany, where in 1517 a priest named Martin Luther wrote his celebrated 95 theses. This document accused the Roman Catholic church of spiritual bankruptcy and monetary corruption. Luther went on to propose a new view of Christianity that rejected many traditional aspects of the religion, principally the priesthood, which he considered a hindrance rather than an aid to the fullest expression of the faith. He envisioned an ideal community of Christians united by conscience and personal piety, free of the official church hierarchy. Luther's radical beliefs quickly traveled through Europe as protestors—or "Protestants"—took up the cry for an overhaul—or "Reformation"—of the established Catholic church.

Religious Strife

For the next 150 years growing discord within the Christian faith threw Europe into turmoil. At first England and Ireland were spared; both countries supported the Catholic church in Rome. But when Pope Clement VII refused to grant England's King Henry VIII a divorce and to sanction his remarriage, Henry switched loyalties. In 1534 he established the Protestant Church of England (the Anglican church), headed by himself.

This action inspired no sympathy in Ireland, which remained firmly Catholic, and the countries found themselves more at odds than ever. The next English monarch, Henry's daughter Elizabeth I, an emphatic opponent of Rome, backed Protestants in several skirmishes, including a violent suppression of Irish Catholics in 1601. After Elizabeth died, in 1603, Ireland remained the target of English hostility as Protestant settlers were sent to Ireland to displace Catholics. In Ulster, the north-

In the 17th century Britain invaded Ireland again, massacring thousands of Catholics.

ernmost province in Ireland, an estimated 30,000 Protestants were slain by Catholic resisters in 1641.

These troubles were magnified by another crisis, the irreconcilable differences pitting England's monarchy against its legislative body, Parliament. Tensions mounted and the country erupted in civil war, which culminated in the beheading of King Charles I in 1649. His replacement, Oliver Cromwell, was a devout Protestant who decided to cure the problem of the Irish once and for all. He organized a military expedition that physically drove the resisters off their land and laid the countryside to ruin. The survivors carried on the struggle until Catholic forces were routed again in the Battle of the Boyne on July 1, 1690.

Once conquered, the Irish lost their autonomy. The English Parliament established the Church of Ireland, which sponsored laws that further disadvantaged Ireland's Catholics. One measure forbade them to purchase land from Protestants unless they first agreed to renounce Catholicism. Another decreed that when a Catholic farmer died his land must be parceled among all his descendants, with

As late as the 19th century, Irish were sharecroppers on land owned by absentee Englishmen.

the result that each inheritor was given a plot too small to farm usefully. As if these indignities were not enough, parochial schools were systematically closed, and Gaelic, Ireland's lovely native language, was banned.

A Naked and Hungry Place

Even as its means of survival dwindled, the Irish population swelled. In the 1830s the number of farm workers and servants doubled, from 665,000 to 1.3 million, most of them living so squalidly that visitors were appalled. George A. T. O'Brien's study, *The Economic History of Ireland from the Union to the Famine*, quotes a Frenchman who toured the Irish countryside in the early 19th century and noted the "pure misery" that characterized the "naked and hungry" place. "I saw the American Indian in his forests," this seasoned observer remarked, "and the black slave in his chains, and I believed that I was seeing in their pitiful condition the most extreme form of human misery; but that was before I knew the lot of poor Ireland."

Misery persisted for generations. By 1700, Irish Catholics owned less than 15 percent of the country's landmass, and by 1755, less than 5 percent. The rest belonged to landlords, many of them living in England. Shunted on to the margins of their own nation, the Irish became "cottiers," farmers huddling as renters on the tiny strips of land they tilled. Millions subsisted exclusively on potatoes, a healthy vegetable that could be grown even in the poorest bog; a family of six sometimes managed for an entire year on a one-acre yield.

The final blow came in 1845 when a fungus disease blanketed Europe's potato fields, causing a

Charles Stewart Parnell led the Home Rule movement in the 1880s.

continental famine that claimed 2.5 million lives. A second crop failure struck in 1846, a third in 1848, and yet another in 1851. Nowhere was the suffering crueler than in Ireland. Potatoes rotted in the ground and in storage bins while starvation reached epidemic proportions. People crazed with hunger ate dogs, cats, and horses, and chewed on grasses torn from barren fields. The truly desperate fed on human corpses. The landscape seemed to echo with the lament composed a century earlier by the poet Egan O'Rahilly:

> All over Ireland—why this chill?
> Why this foul mist?
> Why the crying birds?
> Why do the heavens mutter
> Such wrathful words?

Ireland's population, which had topped 10 million in 1840, tumbled to 6.5 million a decade later, reduced in part by starvation, in part by emigration, as more and more survivors departed for distant lands, mainly the United States and Canada. This trend continued until 1900, when Ireland, alone among European countries, had fewer citizens than it had 100 years before. By 1980 the population had shrunk to 5 million.

Parnell and Home Rule

In the late 19th century, while millions of Irish fled their troubled land, those left behind advanced the cause of a free Irish nation. Oddly enough, this cause profited from the famine, for it was yet another crop failure that spurred the formation of the Irish Land League in 1877, under Michael Davitt.

The Land League organized a successful cottiers' strike on the estate of an absentee English landlord, Captain Charles Cunningham Boycott; similar "boycotts" soon followed.

This activism spawned a number of national leaders in Ireland, chief among them Charles Stewart Parnell, a member of the English Parliament and the charismatic architect of the Irish Home Rule movement. Parnell exhorted Irish peasants to defy their landlords by withholding rent on land that was rightfully theirs.

The British government, worried about Parnell's influence, jailed him in 1881, though he continued to issue directives from behind bars. His release from jail coincided with the brutal murder of two important English magistrates in Dublin's Phoenix Park; though he was personally appalled by the crime, Parnell was blamed for it in some quarters. Five Irishmen were eventually hanged for the murder and Parliament passed an emergency law abolishing jury trials and granting exceptional powers of arrest to the police, while the controversy surrounding Parnell continued to grow.

Parnell's reputation remained untarnished in the eyes of his many followers, however, until he was implicated in a quite different transgression. In 1889 one of his colleagues sued his wife for divorce and publicly named Parnell as her illicit lover. Scandal rocked the British Isles, especially Ireland, where Parnell became the subject of bitter controversy. His opponents argued that Parnell's sexual misconduct confirmed that all along he had been a fraud; his staunch supporters maintained that he had been framed.

Either way, the symbol of Free Ireland was irreparably damaged. Denounced by two crucial

The Easter Rebellion of 1916 left much of Dublin in ruins.

groups—English liberals and the Roman Catholic church—Parnell lost his political strength; before long his health gave out. He died in 1891, a fallen idol. But the achievement of Home Rule remained intact. It had helped dismantle the unchecked power long held in the Irish countryside by Anglo-Irish aristocrats, and it ushered in the transformation of the country into its modern status as a nation of independent land-owning farmers.

Uneasy Truces

Although outbreaks of violence continue to inflame the relationship between Ireland and England, in the 20th century the two countries have consistently worked toward mending their differences. The figure most responsible for this improvement was the great English prime minister, William E. Gladstone (1809–1898). In 1885, under Gladstone's leadership, Parliament broke precedent by making funds available to Ireland's cottiers so they could purchase plots from their landlords at a reasonable cost.

Subsequent acts further enabled Irish farmers to recover the land that had originally belonged to their ancestors. This progress betokened a resurgence of Irish pride: the Gaelic language was again spoken freely and was taught to the young, as were the country's ancient folk traditions.

One theory of revolution holds that violent rebellions occur not when conditions are at their worst, but when they begin to brighten, because improvement whets the public appetite for major reform. This theory helps explain Easter Sunday of 1916, when an army of 2,000 Irishmen took to the streets of Dublin and confronted the British army. Surrounded and overwhelmed, the rebel forces surrendered within a week, and most of the leaders were executed.

Despite this flare-up, the majority of the Irish remained confident that the policy of Home Rule would stay in place. Nonetheless, on January 21, 1919, a political party called *Sinn Fein* (Gaelic for "we ourselves") declared an independent Irish Republic and established an autonomous parliament in Dublin.

Irish Catholics were grateful for the support they received from Irish Americans during the 1921 Civil War.

The English government reacted swiftly, driving Sinn Fein underground, and once more civil war gripped Ireland. In the summer of 1920 savage fighting pitted followers of Sinn Fein against supporters of the British Crown, sometimes dividing families. Stories abounded of atrocities committed in the countryside by Britain's Royal Irish Constabulary, called "Black and Tans" because of their uniforms—khaki tunics and trousers and dark green caps that looked black.

In an attempt to stanch the bloodshed, the English devised a political compromise. In 1921 Ireland was split in two, along lines that still hold. The Irish Free State (known today as the Republic of Ireland) is an independent nation that comprises nearly 90 percent of the land mass and includes 26 counties, with Dublin as its capital. Northern Ireland, or Ulster, comprises six counties and has its capital in Belfast. It remains part of the United Kingdom under the direct control of the English government.

The Celtic Legacy

Like other nations with a tragic history, Ireland has partly compensated for its woes by evolving a remarkably expressive and durable culture. It dates back to the island's first inhabitants, the Celts.

The Celts were originally central European warriors forced out of their own ancient homelands in about 300 B.C. by other competing groups, particularly the Romans and the Germans. Migrating steadily westward, the Celts—or Gauls, as they also are called—swept across the continent, crossed the Channel into England, which they conquered, and continued into Ireland. There they found a lush and sparsely settled countryside and proceeded to establish farming communities, the largest located on man-made islands in Ireland's many lakes and bogs or protected by stone or earthen forts.

While similar European societies were absorbed into the Roman Empire, the Celts remained apart, enclosed by the Irish Sea and ringed by mountains. Thus isolated, Ireland evolved differently from other Western civilizations. As late as the 8th century, it had no single monarch but was splintered into more than 100 small states grouped into five separate kingdoms, each ruled by several powerful families and populated by aristocrats, free farmers, and slaves. And because the country had no comprehensive road system until the 18th century, the Irish stayed remote not only from the rest of Europe, but from each other.

At the same time, Ireland developed a unique set of customs, many revolving around the country's most important activity, farming. An agricultural calendar marked the two main seasons, planting and harvesting. May 1 signaled the completion of sowing and was celebrated with festive events such as the gathering of May flowers and the blessing of children and livestock. The harvest was ushered in with Halloween celebrations that featured a traditional meal of white vegetables — potatoes, cabbage, and turnips.

The most remarkable feature of Celtic culture was a class of men — and possibly a few women — called *Druids*, who have been romanticized by later eras as figures of exceptional, almost magical, powers. Druids were indeed a rare breed, combining many functions: They were storytellers and poets, students of nature and the heavens, philosophers,

Druids, who presided over Celtic culture, were credited with remarkable, even magical, powers.

and moral guides. They also presided over the Celtic religion, a form of pagan worship that attributed mystical qualities to animals, mountains, rivers, and trees, and included unusual rites, sometimes involving human sacrifices, performed in groves and near rivers and lakes. Gradually, the Celtic religion came to be less a system of belief than a storehouse of Irish folklore, filled with elves and pixies and leprechauns. This folk tradition also imbued Gaelic, an unwritten language of enchanting melodiousness and vivid imagery.

Celtic culture was enriched in the 5th century A.D., when Christianity was brought to Ireland from England in the person of St. Patrick. Often called the Apostle of Ireland, he is a figure misted

A bon vivant as well as a genius, Oscar Wilde remains one of Ireland's most celebrated literary figures.

in legend, though his accomplishment is a matter of record—in about A.D. 445 he founded missionary headquarters in Ulster, and within 15 years Ireland had become a Christian nation. Before long Christian Ireland evolved into a major center of learning in Europe. Irish monasteries, renowned for their erudition, sent scholars to the Continent to convert and instruct those who had yet to adopt Christian teachings. English scholars studied at Ireland's schools, fed and housed free of charge.

This passion for learning did not ignore Celtic culture; monks invented the first written form of Gaelic and penned versions of Irish history, laws, poetry, and songs. Today Celtic manuscripts, composed nearly 1,000 years before the advent of the printing press, rank among the glories of that era's art.

Since ancient times the Druids had spun fanciful tales featuring wizardry, beautiful damsels, and exotic settings. The early Christians were equally otherworldly but in a much different way; they favored accounts of religious suffering and renunciation. These opposite points of view merged in the 8th-century masterpiece, *The Book of Kells*, a version of the Gospels punctuated with notes on Irish history. Its pages, exquisitely and lushly ornamented, are prized by art historians. Ireland's unique literary tradition has remained a vital force through the centuries. The most celebrated Irish author is Jonathan Swift (1667–1745), perhaps the finest prose stylist in English, and best known for his satire *Gulliver's Travels*. Later wits include the great playwrights George Bernard Shaw (1856–1950) and Oscar Wilde (1845–1900), whose pungent sallies fill the pages of quotation books.

W. B. Yeats, winner of the 1923 Nobel Prize, wrote some of the century's greatest lyric poetry.

George Bernard Shaw, playwright and social critic, won the Nobel Prize in 1925.

In the 20th century, the outstanding figures are William Butler Yeats (1865–1939), James Joyce (1882–1941), and Samuel Beckett (b.1906). Yeats, a poet, playwright, and student of mysticism, mined the fabular ore of Celtic mythology in his effort to revive the folk tradition. His best poems, such as "The Second Coming," "Among Schoolchildren," and "Sailing to Byzantium," unite the lyrical imagination of Ireland's early inhabitants with a biblical intuition of doom and redemption. Yeats also helped found the Abbey Theatre, a theatrical company devoted to staging native Irish drama.

Yeats's contemporary James Joyce was the most innovative novelist that genre has ever known. Born in Dublin—where all his fiction is set—and educated for the priesthood, Joyce had a remarkable facility for languages and a monkish fascination with categories and forms. His gargantuan novels *Ulysses* and *Finnegans Wake* attempt to fit the wild disorder of human experience into highly structured designs calculated down to the minutest details.

Joyce's protégé, Samuel Beckett, was also born in Dublin, but has mostly written in French, his adopted tongue since the 1950s. Beckett originated "minimalism," a style that uses spare, sometimes simplistic language to convey a mood of anguish and isolation. His most celebrated work, the drama *Waiting for Godot*, written in the ashes of World War II, towers above contemporary theater and has been performed throughout the world.

Ireland's glorious literature offered more than an escape from its tragic history; great Irish authors often commented on the events that seemed to be strangling their land. One of Swift's favorite targets for satire was Ireland's old nemesis, England. Yeats wrote a famous poem, "Easter 1916," lamenting the uprising that cost Ireland so much—and won it so little. And Joyce's first literary effort was "Et tu, Healy!," a poem written when he was nine, vilifying a politician who deserted Parnell.

For many centuries politics, religion, and art have interacted like echoing voices in Ireland, each giving expression to the dire plight of its struggling people. The same medley was repeated in the New World, as immigrant generations and their offspring encountered hardships akin to those that scarred their ancestral land. ✎

The most recent Irish Nobel laureate is Samuel Beckett, awarded the prize in 1969.

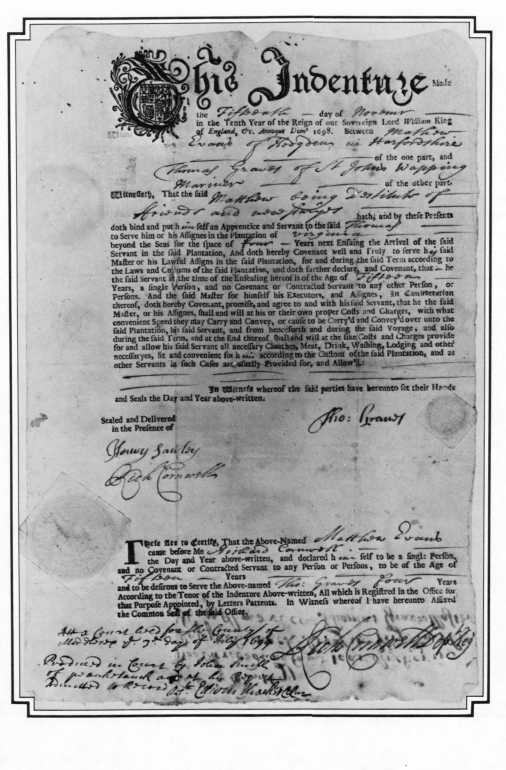

This Indenture Made

the *Fifteenth* — day of *Novemr*
in the Tenth Year of the Reign of our Sovereign Lord *William* King
of England, &c. Annoque Dom' 1698. Between *Mathew*
Evans of Hodgden in Harfordshire
                                    of the one part, and
Thomas Graves of St Johns Wapping
Mariner   of the other part.

Witnesseth, That the said *Matthew being Destitute of*
friends and necessarys hath; and by these Presents
doth bind and put himself an Apprentice and Servant to the said *Thomas*
to Serve him or his Assignes in the Plantation of *virginia*
beyond the Seas for the space of *four* — Years next Ensuing the Arrival of the said
Servant in the said Plantation, And doth hereby Covenant well and Truly to serve the said
Master or his Lawful Assigns in the said Plantation, for and during the said Term according to
the Laws and Customs of the said Plantation, and doth farther declare, and Covenant, that — he
the said Servant at the time of the Ensealing hereof is of the Age of *Fifteen*
Years, a single Person, and no Covenant or Contracted Servant to any other Person, or
Persons. And the said Master for himself his Executors, and Assignes, In Consideration
thereof, doth hereby Covenant, promise, and agree to and with his said Servant, that he the said
Master, or his Assignes, shall and will at his or their own proper Costs and Charges, with what
convenient Speed they may Carry and Convey, or cause to be Carry'd and Convey'd over unto the
said Plantation, his said Servant, and from henceforth and during the said Voyage, and also
during the said Term, and at the End thereof, shall and will at the like Costs and Charges provide
for and allow his said Servant all necessary Cloathes, Meat, Drink, Washing, Lodging and other
necessaryes, fit and convenient for him according to the Custom of the said Plantation, and as
other Servants in such Cases are usually Provided for, and Allow'd:

_____

                    In Witness whereof the said parties have hereunto set their Hands
and Seals the Day and Year above-written.

Sealed and Delivered
in the Presence of   *Tho: Graves*

Henry Sandley

Rich Cornwell

These Are to Certify, That the Above-Named *Matthew Evans*
came before Me *Richard Cornwell* ————
the Day and Year above-written, and declared him self to be a single Person,
and no Covenant or Contracted Servant to any Person or Persons, to be of the Age of
Fifteen Years
and to be desirous to Serve the Above-named *Tho: Graves four* Years
According to the Tenor of the Indenture Above-written, All which is Registred in the Office for
that Purpose Appointed, by Letters Pattents. In Witness whereof I have hereunto Affixed
the Common Seal of the said Office.

Att a Court held for the County of
Middlesex the 3d day of July 1699   *Rich Cornwell Dep Reg*

Produced in Court by John Snell
of Wankland and at his Request
Admitted to Record pr Edm Heath Clr

*In the 18th century indentured
servants contracted for a specified
term of service, in this instance
four years.*

THE
NEW
WORLD

Although Irish migration to North America peaked in the mid- to late-19th century, the Irish had been coming to the New World in substantial numbers since the colonial era of the 18th century. The first immigrants included farmers and laborers, landless peasants, military and political prisoners deported by their government, and religious dissenters. The vast majority were poor and, surprisingly, tended not to be Catholic. They belonged instead to an altogether different category called Scotch-Irish.

The Ulsterians

Today's Scotch-Irish Americans are descendants of people removed from Scotland in the 17th century by the English, who sent them to Ulster, where they were expected to establish Protestantism. They had a bad time of it in Northern Ireland, however, often suffering discrimination, and in the 18th century an estimated 250,000 departed for America, settling at first in New England.

Charles Carroll was the only Catholic to sign the Declaration of Independence.

Many of these immigrants paid for their passage by contracting out as indentured servants, that is, as hirelings required to repay the costs of their transatlantic journey by working for a specified length of time, usually as menial farmhands. It was a condition scarcely better than enslavement, and some indentured servants reacted by running away, vanishing into the frontier wilds where their masters had little hope of tracking them down. Newspapers such as Benjamin Franklin's *Pennsylvania Gazette* were filled with advertisements offering rewards for the return of runaways, many of whom bore Irish names.

Those who stuck out their term of servitude, normally about seven years, often fled the New England colonies. A popular destination was the Appalachian Mountains, where they became subsistence farmers, rather like the majority of Irish who remained in Ireland. Others went farther south, to Maryland, Virginia, the Carolinas, and Georgia.

These immigrants belonged to the Irish Protestant—or Presbyterian—church, and brought to the New World a form of piety that still bore the imprint of Martin Luther. They attended Sabbath services that were long, severe, and strictly observed. The somber tone of those services echoed in the home, where such frivolities as theater, dancing, and card playing were frowned upon or forbidden. Presbyterian beliefs influenced other denominations of American Protestants, though their traces exist only faintly in the practices of contemporary Presbyterians.

One feature of Presbyterianism was an English legacy—extreme antipathy toward Catholics—that through the 18th century overrode the democratic principles of the colonies, some of which denied Catholics the vote. In addition, Catholics were castigated in propaganda routinely spread by ministers, teachers, and newspaper publishers. In most colonies—even Maryland, designated as a Catholic haven by its founder, Lord Baltimore—the minority religion could be observed only with great discretion. As late as the Revolutionary War, only about 25,000 Catholics lived in America, compared with almost 3.5 million Protestants.

Nonetheless, prejudice in America was less severe than in Ireland, and some prominent Irish Catholics figured in early American history. One example is Charles Carroll III of Carrollton, Maryland, the only Catholic to sign the Declaration of Independence. Another is Thomas Fitzsimmons, the only Catholic whose signature graces the Constitution. Fitzsimmons lived in Philadelphia, one of the first American cities to attract a sizable Irish-Catholic population; by 1880 the city had 6,000 Irish Catholics, making it the largest such community in North America.

At this time, many Irish immigrated to Canada, which had even more unclaimed land than the American colonies. The government of Canada—or British North America—was eager to send new arrivals to out-of-the-way areas, so Irish immigrants joined other newcomers from the British Isles on the pioneer trek north and west.

They were aided in this adventure by land companies, which received large grants of territory from the government with the stipulation that they attract settlers whom they assisted by building roads and providing services. The biggest of these land companies, the Canada Company, had obtained 2.4 million acres by 1830. A steady flow of pioneers staked claims in New Brunswick and farther north, following waterways such as the Saint John and Ottawa rivers, then fanning out along the shore. The northern shores of the Great Lakes, especially Ontario, Erie, and Huron, became major settlement areas.

It was not only land companies that arranged for immigrant settlements in Canada. In the Maritime Provinces—Nova Scotia, New Brunswick, and Prince Edward Island—modest communities were often set up by individual entrepreneurs. One of the best known was Colonel Thomas Talbot, who between 1812 and 1837 had populated the shore of Lake Erie with 50,000 pioneers. Another agent, Peter Robinson, a native Canadian, brought 2,000 immigrants over from Ireland in 1825 and established them in 5 communities north of Lake Ontario.

Once they arrived, these settlers faced a difficult task. They had to cut down trees, build cabins, scrounge up farm animals, and provide for immediate needs such as food and clothing. It took 3 years, on average, to clear 30 acres, which meant that towns grew slowly. Between 1815 and 1850, however, hundreds of small communities—each with several mills, a few stores, and a school that often doubled as a church—had sprung up, enough to usher in a new era of commerce and transportation. In that same period, Canada's population more than tripled, reaching 2.3 million in 1851.

The Other Irish

The first of the "other Irish" immigrants—Irish Catholics—actually landed in Canada, some of them as early as the 17th century because of ties

between southern Ireland and France, a Catholic nation which then ruled much of Canada. In fact 5 percent of "New France" was Irish, as was a large portion of Newfoundland, the island province off the mainland coast.

These newcomers had a rough time; most worked as fishermen, faring no better than they had as laborers or tenant farmers in Ireland. Even after Canada's economy expanded in the 19th century, offering new opportunities to immigrants, few of those from Ireland could afford to travel across the enormous country. Most clung to the eastern provinces.

Meanwhile Irish Catholics had begun to arrive in the United States in large numbers. Three hundred thousand had already immigrated in the years between 1800 and 1830, and in the following decade, when the failure of the potato crop devastated Ireland, the numbers swelled. Between 1846 and 1851, more than 1 million Irish—almost all destitute and downtrodden—crossed the Atlan-

American ships offered immigrants better accommodations—at a price higher than most could afford.

The agonies of steerage have become part of American lore.

tic, and even after the blight lifted, huge numbers kept coming. Lured by the encouraging news they received from immigrants in the New World, an estimated 873,000 Irish arrived between 1860 and 1880, and a million more would follow during the next 20 years.

Most of them weathered the Atlantic crossing in steerage—inferior, often wretched accommodations reserved for the lowest-paying passengers. For $50, no small sum for an impoverished immigrant, passengers were crammed into a cargo ship with as many as 900 others, allotted only as much space as their bodies took up, their possessions tightly rolled up by their sides. Worse, filth and human excrement were everywhere. And cholera and other fatal illnesses, often brought on board by diseased immigrants, stalked the ship like a stowaway.

Stephen deVere, a wealthy Irishman so curious about steerage conditions that he decided to experience them first-hand, set down his impressions in his *Journal*, quoted in Terry Coleman's *Going to America*:

> Before the emigrant has been a week at sea he is
> an altered man. How can it be otherwise? Hundreds
> of poor people, men, women, and children, of all
> ages, from the drivelling idiot of ninety to the
> babe just born, huddled together without light,
> without air, wallowing in filth and breathing a
> fetid atmosphere, sick in body, dispirited in heart,
> the fevered patient lying . . . in sleeping places so
> narrow as almost to deny them the power of
> indulging, by a change of position, the natural
> restlessness of their diseases; by the agonized
> raving disturbing those around, and predisposing
> them through the effects of the imagination, to
> imbibe the contagion; living without food or
> medicine . . . dying without the voice of spiritual
> consolation, and burying in the deep without the
> rites of the church.

Scores of similar accounts survive, each describing a nightmare that lasted from one to three months. Although the American and English governments enacted laws meant to improve conditions, it was difficult to enforce them, and steerage passengers traveled at the mercy of captain, crew, and each other. Forced to share berths, men and women had little or no privacy. The standard meal consisted of rough grain, served as a hardened lump. Crew members cursed passengers and sometimes physically abused them.

By the end of one 1853 voyage that began with 200 passengers, between 37 and 41 had died en route. Their corpses were heaved overboard. On the whole, though, immigrants arrived safely; death claimed on the average about one out of two hundred passengers, decidedly better odds than those posed by the Great Famine.

In one respect the burden of traveling steerage was eased: The cost of the voyage was often shouldered by existing communities of Irish North Americans who financed the emigration of relatives and friends through organizations such as Boston's *Pilot* newspaper and New York's Emigrant Industrial Savings Bank. And in 1871 an international postal money-order agreement, signed by the American and British governments, aided the transfer of funds between nations. From 1848 to 1900 Irish North Americans sent an annual average of $5 million to Ireland, 90 percent of it from the United States.

The New Troubles

The vast majority of 19th-century Irish Catholic immigrants soon discovered, however, that conditions in America were little better than those they had escaped, particularly in the cities. In contrast with other newcomers—Scandinavians and Ger-

Arrivals in New York Harbor were logged in and examined by physicians.

mans, for instance—the Irish seldom lit out for the unpopulated frontier. One reason was that the land had been a source of anguish in Ireland, especially after the recent crop failures. In addition, most Irish farmers had experience growing only one crop, potatoes, and were ill-equipped to try their hands at others. Finally, Irish were reluctant to venture into isolated areas barren of churches and other places where they were used to congregating.

Huge numbers of Irish immigrants were thus lumped together in industrial and port cities. In the mid-19th century four states—Massachusetts, New York, Pennsylvania, and Illinois—contained more than half the total Irish American population. Penniless and unskilled, these refugees from a land racked by starvation took whatever jobs they could find, for any wage. In the 1830s unskilled laborers received about $1.00 per working day. A decade later, even as business boomed, wages dropped to less than 75 cents for a 10- or 12-hour working day.

The situation erupted in 1844, when a bitter feud divided Philadelphia's weavers, most of whom toiled at home on commission from merchants. Irish Catholics objected to what they felt were exploitative conditions and went on strike, without the support of Protestant weavers, who continued

In 1844 a feud dividing Philadelphia's weavers erupted into violence.

to work as before. When angry Catholics attacked the home of a Protestant nonstriker, destroying his work and equipment, the struggle took on denominational overtones. In Charlestown, Massachusetts, "nativists," believers in the intrinsic inferiority of all immigrants, burned a Catholic convent to the ground. Eventually, the violence cooled, and the strike ended.

A similar fate befell Irish immigrants to Canada, of whom there were 90,000 in 1847. Their numbers rose so dramatically that by 1871 Irish Canadians were the most populous ethnic group in every city and major town except French Montreal and Quebec City. This situation was short-lived, however. Prospects were so limited that most of the immigrants migrated again—to the United

States. By the 1860s thousands had made this second journey, and the trend continued into the 20th century. Today only Saint John, the capital of Newfoundland, and Protestant Ontario, known as the "Belfast of America," have large Irish-Canadian communities.

Those who joined the Irish in America found that cities there were bigger, jobs more numerous, and that the United States was an independent nation, free of British rule. Even so, conditions were grim. Because there were no unions in those days, laborers had no leverage to combat exploitative employers, and the sudden influx of foreigners willing to accept any wage panicked native workers who were already underpaid. In New York City, the main port of entry for newcomers, Irish immigrants took the blame for lowering wages, which declined during these years despite an enormous leap in merchants' profits.

The Constitutional separation of church and state seemed threatened by the advent of Irish Catholics, represented by a cathedral in this Thomas Nast cartoon.

The Irish-American Church

The nation at this time was overwhelmingly Protestant, and anti-Catholicism inevitably became the battle cry of political factions. The 1840s and 1850s saw the rise of the American party, whose bland title disguised a policy of discrimination against anyone who was not white, Anglo-Saxon, and Protestant. Popularly called the Know-Nothing party—because its members, when asked about their secret intentions, invariably replied "I know nothing"—this group singled out Catholics, especially those from Ireland.

Irish-American funding of charity hospitals continued into the 20th century.

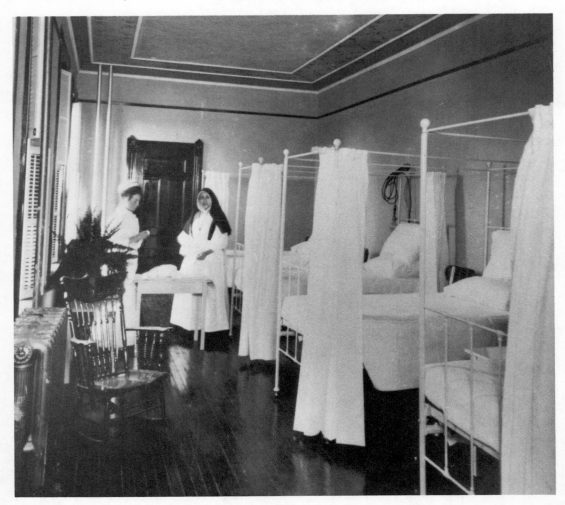

Less radical Americans also found Catholicism suspect, for several reasons. For one, Protestants thought that the church hierarchy, still centered in Rome and presided over by the pope, smacked of the same corruption that had inspired Luther's revolt. Just as importantly, the church required that religious loyalty precede national patriotism in the thinking of its members, a priority that intensified the suspicions directed at immigrants who were already perceived as aliens.

At first these suspicions were justified. The staunch Irish Catholics who arrived in North America in the 1840s and 1850s believed that governments should be subordinate to the church, that Catholicism was the only true faith, and that all others were sinners if they failed to convert. So narrow a view, at odds with the freethinking principles at the core of American democracy, alarmed a Protestant majority already walled in by distrust.

Gradually, however, Irish Americans molded their religious outlook into conformity with the prevailing values of the New World. Without lessening its spiritual loyalty to Rome, the American Catholic church began to adapt to the new moral climate, less out of a desire to placate Protestants than out of necessity; as the rallying point for nearly all Irish Catholics, the churches had no choice but to become all-purpose community centers for immigrants.

For Irish Americans, the local church not only offered sanctuary from prejudice; it also helped immigrants ease into the larger society by mediating between Irish traditions and American customs. The parish priest, in particular, became an important symbol. In urban slums and the frontier towns where a few bold immigrants ventured, priests served as educators, healers, and counselors, and also supervised hospitals, asylums, and orphanages, often staffed by Irish nuns. In Europe the ideal priest had been a monastic figure devoted to the spiritual side of his calling, someone to be revered because he had renounced the temptations that brought about the downfall of lesser men. But in America a new kind of priest was emerging, equally chaste but more worldly, even activist, someone who could fend for himself on a dangerous street corner or a rough western outpost, who could stand up to a bully and also invoke the lessons of Christian brotherhood.

In the mid-19th century, there was a growing feeling among church leaders that because the little formal religious education available to Roman Catholics was confined mostly to classes in church basements, Irish-American children were not being adequately taught the tenets of the Catholic faith. Furthermore, the first immigrants from Ireland had been so concerned with putting food on the table that they often sent the entire family off to work, and children received almost no education in the basic skills of reading, writing, and arithmetic. But as Irish Americans grew more secure in their new surroundings and began thinking of advancement, education took on new importance.

In the 1830s and 1840s these twin needs led to a series of fund-raising campaigns in Irish neighborhoods in cities such as New York and Boston designed to establish a comprehensive system of parochial schools, one per parish. Poor families willingly contributed the few pennies they could spare in the hope that their children would be ed-

(continued on page 57)

THE CELTIC LEGACY

In The Book of Kells, an 8th-century masterpiece, the infant Christ is swaddled in the same lush green that today surrounds Menlo Castle, a medieval ruin located in the western county of Galway.

Dublin's varied cultural life
includes the Abbey Theatre,
founded in 1902, and the
fiction of James Joyce, who
paid tribute to his native city
even after he migrated to
continental Europe.

The Irish-American flair for performance flourished a century ago in vaudeville and thrives today on the Broadway stage, where Eugene O'Neill's classic The Iceman Cometh *was* recently revived.

The best-known Irish-American holiday is St. Patrick's Day, celebrated every March 17. In New York City the spectacle attracts such honorary Celts as Mayor Edward I. Koch; in Chicago, the Illinois River becomes an emerald waterway.

The mystique of the Kennedys—America's "first family"—spans several generations of grand accomplishment and high tragedy.

Parochial schools angered
many 19th-century
Americans, who distrusted
the influence of Catholicism
in the classroom.

(continued from page 48)

ucated in an environment free of the prejudice so common in public classrooms.

These early parochial schools concentrated on guiding children toward Catholicism but away from the Old World culture that still ruled in the home. Instruction in patriotism and religion supplemented the basic curriculum: less attention was paid to the imaginative side of learning. A century later this pragmatic approach still dictated Catholic education: boys were taught to be devout and also to acquire skills that would find them decent jobs; girls were trained to become wives and mothers.

This network of parochial schools reflected the changing leadership of the American Catholic church, which by 1850 was becoming increasingly dominated by the Irish. Between 1840 and 1850 the total number of priests rose dramatically, from 480 to 1,500, and one third of them were Irish. In 1875, John McCloskey, the son of Irish immigrants, became the first American cardinal of Irish descent. A quarter of a century later, more than three fourths of the nation's cardinals and more than half its bishops were of Irish descent.

So powerful had Irish Americans become in the American Catholic church that other groups began to protest. In the 1890s German and Italian Catholics petitioned the Vatican to appoint their own bishops and, in effect, to establish separate Catholic churches throughout the United States.

Irish Americans objected strenuously to these demands, in part because control of the American

New York City's Altar Boys' Association singled out gifted students often headed for the priesthood.

church meant access to political power. The centralized hierarchy of cardinals, bishops, and priests served to further social goals. Parishioners who reliably attended Sunday mass could be counted on to back the church's view on public issues and to vote as a solid block on election day. The partnership between Irish-American politicians and servants of the church usually produced results satisfactory to both.

This relationship has weakened in our own day owing to a sharp decline in church attendance and to the dwindling numbers of young men entering the priesthood. There is evidence, as well, that even devout Catholics are less willing to obey Church teachings than their forebears were, particularly on the issue of birth control.

Nonetheless, many Irish-American cardinals and bishops still exercise power that is political in nature. In New York City, for example, where the Catholic archdiocese has consistently wielded considerable influence in the 20th century, John Cardinal O'Connor often comments on political issues and continues the tradition of forceful Irish-Catholic leadership.

The role assumed in the United States by the Catholic church is an ideal instance of an Old World institution taking root in the New World and adjusting in a way that kept traditional values alive. But it was only the first step that Irish immigrants took in the grand project of becoming Americans. ❧

BATTLEFIELDS OF ASSIMILATION

The great Irish immigrant tide of the 1840s and 1850s came at a pivotal moment in American history. The country, after three quarters of a century of independence, had outgrown its colonial beginnings; the towering shadow of England had shrunk, and Americans were eager to expand the nation's southern and western borders and to iron out regional differences that increasingly were dividing an otherwise united people.

The Spoils of War

Since the early 19th century, the American government had sought a means of obtaining Texas, repeatedly offering to purchase the vast area—larger than France—from Mexico. Despite spurning all offers, Mexico encouraged the immigration of Americans, who steadily crossed the border to plant cotton and clear room for ranches.

These settlers were officially living on foreign soil but considered themselves U.S. citizens. They resisted the rule of the Mexican Republic, not least

In March 1863 Irish Americans battled government troops in the streets of New York City.

because it forbade plantation owners to use slave labor. Although special privileges were extended to American colonies such as Austin, where Anglos outnumbered the native population, Texas agitated for independence and achieved it in 1836 by defeating Mexico in battle.

Most Texans wanted the region to become part of the United States, but the country was equally divided between free and slave states, and Texas would upset the balance. In 1845, U.S. president John Tyler, on his last day in office, secured the admission of Texas to the Union as the 28th state. Mexico protested and war broke out, lasting until 1848. Fully half the soldiers in the United States Army were recent immigrants, most of them Irish and German volunteers who saw the war as an opportunity to earn a steady wage and to escape the dreary life of the slums.

Undoubtedly, those immigrants who served in the war improved the group's overall status. Irish Catholics, long suspected of being more loyal to the church than to their adopted country, benefited from the chance to prove their bravery and patriotism.

A far more massive undertaking, the Civil War (1861–1865), had the same effect. Most Irish Americans still lived in the Northeast or the Midwest, and both regions sided with the Union, to whose army the group contributed enormously—an estimated 200,000 Irish natives joined its ranks. New York sent an Irish Brigade to the conflict, as did Pennsylvania, Ohio, Indiana, Illinois, and Iowa.

Many Irish-born soldiers were decorated or promoted, and tales abounded of their heroics. Eight Irishmen rose to the rank of general in the

Union army. The Confederacy had five generals of Irish, or more likely Scotch-Irish descent. On both sides, Irishmen won recognition as fierce fighters. Edward Wakin's *Enter the Irish American* quotes an account of the first battle of Bull Run, in which Union general William Tecumseh Sherman

> turned and called to his Irish. It was a medieval moment—long lines of men on scarlet knees in green grass . . . a strange green banner above them . . . bayonets glittering like spears above their bowed heads . . . Latin words rolling from the lips of every soul to God. The benediction done, the men put on their caps, and as they rose Captain Thomas F. Meagher . . . standing in front, ran his eyes up and down the line and then in fond challenge cried, "Come on, boys, you've got your chance at last."

Anarchy on the Streets

The Civil War was also the occasion of a shameful episode in Irish-American history. In March 1863, Congress sought to strengthen depleted Union

Most Irish Americans were trapped in urban neighborhoods such as New York City's Five Points.

forces by passing the first national draft law, which called for all able-bodied men between the ages of 20 and 45 to serve a 3–year term, unless they found a substitute or paid the government $300. Many Irishmen welcomed the economic opportunity offered by the war, but for others the draft seemed to reinforce unjust social distinctions—having money meant avoiding the front. In New York City, outraged Irish vented their frustration in an outbreak of violence irrationally directed against the city's black community, which numbered only 10,000, no match for a mob of 200,000. By the time federal troops established control, after 4 days of anarchy, 1,200 people had been killed or seriously injured and Manhattan's Colored Orphan Asylum had been burned to the ground.

This incident served as a warning that cities were becoming the crucible of Irish unrest. The great majority of Irish Americans were trapped in slums far worse than those that corrode the urban

Young children usually worked at an early age, often on the street.

landscape today. Nineteenth-century cities had yet to evolve workable ordinances safeguarding living conditions, and the poor lacked the political clout to improve their lot. Crowded into filthy and unsafe tenements, they suffered from high rates of infant mortality, accidental death, and fatal disease, especially in New York, where housing remained unspeakable for decades.

The English novelist Charles Dickens, whose fame rested partly on his crusading protests against the conditions of London's inner city, was led on a tour of Manhattan's Five Points Slum in 1842. In *American Notes* he described what he saw:

Sing Sing prison, in upstate New York, held a high percentage of Irish-American inmates.

> What place is this, to which the squalid street conducts us? A kind of square of leprous houses, some of which are attainable only by crazy wooden stairs. . . . Here, too, are lanes and alleys, paved with mud knee-deep: underground chambers, where they dance and game; the walls bedecked rough designs of ships, and forts, and flags, and American Eagles out of number: ruined houses, open to the street, whence, through wide gaps in the walls, other ruins loom upon the eye, as though the world of vice and misery had nothing else to show: hideous tenements which take their name from robbery and murder; all [that] is loathsome, drooping, and decayed is here.

Another visitor gave a careful description of a tenement in the same neighborhood. Its basement, he reported, contained a barroom and a dance hall, with extra beds for temporary lodgers. Upstairs, conditions recalled the indignities of steerage; 75 people were crammed into 12 airless rooms at a cost of $4 per month, about a week's wages and a dollar more than the rent paid by the residents in

Laying track for the transcontinental railroad helped these Irish Americans escape city slums.

the rear of the building who inhabited subdivided wooden hovels.

A worse problem was filth. There was no indoor plumbing or running water, and sewage piled up in backyard privies, festering there until authorities got around to clearing it up. By then rats had already gathered, spreading disease. The victims were most often children. By the age of six, many were practically living in the streets, sweeping crossings, hawking apples, newspapers, or matches, and begging and stealing. John Francis Maguire's *The Irish in America*, published in 1868, included observations such as this:

> No one can walk the length of Broadway without
> meeting some hideous troop of ragged girls,
> from twelve years down, brutalized almost beyond
> redemption by premature vice, clad in the filthy
> refuse of the rag pickers; collections, obscene
> of speech, the stamp of childhood gone from their
> faces, hurrying along with harsh laughter and
> foulness on their lips that some of them have
> learned by rote, yet too young to understand it;
> with thief written in their cunning eyes and whore
> on their depraved faces.

Disease shrouded the tenements. In New York a typhoid epidemic swept the Irish community in 1837; typhus hit in 1842, cholera in 1849, and tuberculosis and pneumonia—often fatal ailments in that primitive era of medical science—were a constant threat. From 1849 to 1859, 85 percent of all the foreign-born patients admitted to Manhattan's Bellevue Hospital were Irish. In 1857, two thirds of the city's total deaths claimed children less than five years old, most of them Irish.

The toll all this took on the social life of Irish Americans was devastating, and the community resorted to whatever solace they could find. A popular anesthetic was alcohol, an age-old addiction in Ireland that made its way to the New World, killing a great many immigrants. Others succumbed to equally alarming temptations. Of the 1,200 foreign-born prostitutes in New York City, two thirds came from Ireland. And in 1865, nearly one half of New York's total prison population, or about 20,000 inmates, were Irish-born. Organizations tried to relieve these problems. Antialcohol societies formed in big northeastern cities, and groups such as New York's Irish Emigrant Society tried to steer newcomers away from the illegal or unsavory enticements of the ghetto.

The rest of the Irish-American community fared little better. Most of its members remained marooned in the lower classes. Few learned crafts, and fewer still became teachers, clerks, or professionals. Men usually found work as day laborers, porters, or bartenders; many women and girls became domestics, cleaning homes and caring for the families of the well-to-do.

On the whole, Irish immigrants climbed less rapidly up the social ladder than Germans or Scan-

By the late 19th century, Irish shanty towns, such as this one in New York City, had sprung up nationwide.

dinavians, the other most populous immigrant groups of the time. Indeed studies have equated the rate of Irish social progress in the 19th century with that of blacks, a shocking comparison given that blacks had been chained into slavery for more than a century.

The Pioneer Spirit

One reason the Irish seemed doomed to squalid conditions was the deep aversion many of them felt toward rural life as a result of the Great Famine, which had turned Ireland's farm country into a barren wasteland. Even though the best hope for the future often lay in the frontier, with its vast unclaimed spaces, only about 10 percent of the immigrant Irish chose to make their fortunes there.

The situation was such that efforts were organized to lure immigrants into rural areas. Those who ventured forth drifted into various kinds of employment: some worked on the canals and the railroad and in the mines; some drove cattle; others joined the forces of law or those opposing it; a few even rode with Custer. The 1849 gold rush attracted so many Irish to California that by 1870 they constituted the largest foreign-born group in the state.

Many Irish who helped build the nation's transcontinental network of railroads wound up living in shanty communities, called Irishtowns, that sprang up alongside the tracks. Upstate New York had several Irishtowns, and enclaves settled also in the Midwest. According to the 1860 census the Irish were the most numerous foreign-born group in the United States in many cities, including Boston; Providence; New Haven; Philadelphia; Pitts-

James Clare Flood, an Irish American who made a fortune mining silver in the 1860s, built a palatial house in Menlo Park, California.

burgh; Washington, D.C.; New Orleans; San Francisco; and Savannah.

These were successful times for some Irish Americans. A few made millions mining the fabled Comstock Lode, an enormous deposit of silver and gold discovered in Nevada in 1859. Others rose to the top of state governments in both Nevada and California.

By the turn of the century San Francisco's exclusive Nob Hill was filled with mansions owned by successful Irish such as James Phelan, who began as a saloon keeper, later became a banker, and by 1870 was one of the 10 richest men in the city. Another grand house belonged to Peter Donahue, whose company erected San Francisco's first streetlights. Donahue eventually owned a steamboat line, organized a railroad company, and left a $4–million estate when he died. Phelan and Donahue were rare exceptions, however. Most Irish Americans remained on the East Coast, clustered in poor neighborhoods they had little prospect of leaving. ⚒

THE GREATEST FREAK ON RECO

Political patronage boosted many Irish Americans into municipal police forces.

GAINING A VOICE

As the 19th century drew to a close, the growing population of Irish Americans still found themselves at the bottom of the social heap, particularly in the cities, where most continued to live. There were signs of progress, of course—the swells perched regally on the San Francisco hills, the miners who struck gold, and others who had the talent or luck to rise above the common lot.

For the rest, progress came by inches and as the result of group effort. The main instrument for advancement was politics, which not only opened the way for individual immigrants but also brought about major social changes that benefited the entire community and the country as a whole.

The Political Arena

America's democratic process gave Irish Americans the opportunity to call on political skills developed over centuries of strife in Ireland. At first Irish Americans directed their political efforts toward assisting the beleaguered land they had forsaken. From the 1820s to the 1840s, the dynamic Irishman Daniel O'Connell succeeded in soliciting money and support for his campaign to disrupt relations between the United States and Great Britain. Later, the Irish Republican Brotherhood, better known as the *Fenians*, splintered into different factions that promoted rival solutions to the problem of asserting Ireland's independence from England. One group staged a hapless uprising in Ireland; another invaded Canada, a focus of enmity because of its allegiance to England.

Irish Americans employed less extreme tactics when commenting on political issues rooted in their new country. In urban centers they turned their numerical strength to advantage, gaining control first of the Democratic party and then of City Hall. Many refugees from the Great Famine set up efficient, and sometimes corrupt, political machines that reliably delivered the Irish-Catholic vote on election day.

Like the Roman Catholic church, political organizations boosted Irish immigrants into the mainstream of American society. In return for their loyalty to the Democratic party, Irish Americans were rewarded with jobs, food, and legal assistance. And as Irish Americans took charge of the Democratic party, they stamped it with distinct characteristics imported from across the Atlantic: loyalty, respect for elders, and willingness to serve.

In Philadelphia, New York, Boston, Chicago, and half a dozen smaller cities, Irish neighborhoods produced ambitious politicians who parlayed community needs into opportunities for fattening their wallets and accruing personal power. As more and more Irish Americans climbed into elective and ap-

Another election victory is celebrated at Tammany Hall.

The Molly Maguires met secretly to plot against mine owners.

pointive offices, the organizations that backed them took on an unsavory cast. Political machines such as New York City's Tammany Hall often conspired with dishonest politicians and businessmen and even with the criminal underworld.

When William Marcy "Boss" Tweed, the notorious kingpin of Tammany Hall, went to jail in 1873, his successor "Honest" John Kelly became the first of a continuing line of Irishmen to dominate New York's backroom politics. Soon the system of unelected bosses spread to other cities, with Irishmen at or near the top.

This was the "Gilded Age" of America's rich and powerful, a time when dishonesty in national and state politics swelled to epic proportions. Some have called it the "Great Barbecue" because a few powerful figures feasted at the expense of the majority. The public had become so jaded by it all that when one of Wall Street's many swindlers was at last nabbed, he could cheerfully reply, "Nothing is lost save honor."

By comparison big-city machines seemed almost virtuous; Tammany Hall, for example, aided countless needy dependents at a time when government itself had not yet begun to provide any of the health, legal, and employment services we now take for granted. George Washington Plunkett, a Tammany district leader, once gave a clear explanation of the Irish-American political philosophy, quoted in William L. Riordan's *Plunkett of Tammany Hall*:

If a family is burned out [of their home], I don't ask whether they are Republicans or Democrats, and I don't refer them to the Charity Organization Service which would investigate their case in a month or two and decide if they were worthy of help 'bout the time are dead from starvation. I just get living quarters for them, buy clothes for them if their clothes were burned up, and fix them till they get things runnin' again. It's philanthropy but it's [also] politics—mighty good politics. Who can tell how many votes one of these fires brings me?

Were the rewards corrupt? Plunkett admitted as much. "Many of our men have grown rich in politics," he said. "I have myself . . . and I'm getting richer every day. . . . There's an honest graft, and I'm an example of how it works. . . . I seen opportunities and took 'em."

The Unions

At about the same time the Irish began their involvement in politics, they also sought to reform a domain where they had long been victimized—the workplace. In this area, however, there was no built-in system, such as electoral politics, which they could use to build a power base. Industrial America remained in the grip of the "bosses," a select few of whom—tycoons such as Jay Gould, John D. Rockefeller, and Cornelius Vanderbilt—ruled like monarchs, unchecked by even minimal restrictions governing business practices.

As unjust as this state of affairs seems today, it had the endorsement of many Americans. The alternative, government regulation of business, was perceived as a hindrance to the great strides the country was making toward becoming an important industrial nation, on a par with England and Germany. For many citizens, including those struggling to climb out of the gutter, the celebrated "captains of industry" (or "robber barons," as their detractors labeled them) seemed like unique American heroes who had set an example others could follow.

But there was another, darker side to the economic bonanza, the side inhabited by those who toiled in the mines and mills, the oil fields and smelting houses, on which the great fortunes were erected. Just as there were no individual or corporate taxes restricting profits, there also were no laws protecting common wage earners. Workers put in 10- and 12-hour days, 6 days a week, and had no means of protesting even the worst conditions. This state of affairs gave birth to the trade union movement, beginning in the 1870s and lasting until the 1930s, when the Great Depression forced government to begin large-scale regulation of the economy.

From the outset Irish Americans, excluded from the inner sanctums of the financial elite, enlisted with the cause of organized labor and found themselves in the thick of bloody battles. In San Francisco, for example, the Workingmen's party, better known as the "Wild Irish," led an attack not on the employers who exploited them but on Chinese immigrants, whom they accused of stealing their jobs. And on the other side of the continent, in Pennsylvania, Irish-American coal miners were embroiled in an equally violent labor tragedy.

Pennsylvania's anthracite coal mines were a dangerous and demoralizing place to work. They earned their owners large profits but offered little

In 1886 the Knights of Labor included a delegation of women.

Dancing classes groomed Irish Americans for entrance into polite society.

reward for the men who actually labored in the pits, many of them Irish immigrants or their sons. Their sentiments were made clear in this mining song cited in Lawrence J. McCaffrey's *The Irish Diaspora in America*:

Sucking up the coal dust into your lungs,
Underneath the hills where there is no sun
Trying to make a living on a dollar a day,
Digging bloody coal in Pennsylvania.

Fed up with brutalizing conditions, Irish Americans formed a secret society named after an antilandlord organization in Ireland, the Molly Maguires. They retaliated against owners by dynamiting mines, assassinating at least nine foremen, and spreading terror throughout the countryside. Finally a detective hired by the owners infiltrated the group and identified the conspirators in a courtroom. Twenty Irishmen were hanged, the secret society was broken, and drudgery in the mines continued as before.

Less extreme protestors attempted to work within the democratic system to bring about reform. In the late 1860s Martin Burke took over the American Miners' Association, and before long other labor leaders emerged, such as William McLaughlin of the Shoemakers Union and J. P. McDonnell of the International Labor Union. But progress came slowly, in part because of fallout from the Molly Maguires and in part because many labor leaders misunderstood the implications of industrialization. Terence V. Powderly, for instance, head of the Knights of Labor, believed that most workers would abandon their industrial jobs as soon as they could afford to become independent farmers. He failed to realize that wage-and-hour labor had become permanent fixtures of the American economy.

Powderly's Knights of Labor foundered in the 1880s, but other Irishmen continued the struggle. By 1900, according to the *Harvard Encyclopedia of American Ethnic Groups*, "Irish immigrants or their descendants held the presidencies of over 50 of the 110 unions in the American Federation of Labor." The reigning view of the trade union movement favored "gradualism," an approach that used the existing free enterprise system to achieve small but clear-cut gains in wages and working conditions. This modified approach has been adopted by most of the Irish Americans who have since become prominent union leaders.

Many Irish Americans worked for the well-to-do as domestic servants.

Winning Acceptance

Even as the 20th century drew near, Irish Americans still carried the burden of prejudice from the Protestant majority. In the 1890s the American Protective Association revived the nativist agenda of their political forebears, the Know-Nothings. "No Irish need apply" notices were a common sight, as were signs in hotels and restaurants reading "No Irish Permitted in this Establishment." Newspaper caricatures gloried in the popular image of the typical Irishman: stupid, brutish, drunk, prone to violence, and slavishly obedient to the pope.

This crude stereotype gradually faded as Irish Americans ascended the job ladder. Many found work in the area of municipal service, becoming policemen, firemen, and civil servants. But despite these gains, 42 percent of working Irish Americans in 1890 were servants, and many others were unskilled laborers. Less than one tenth of 1 percent of Boston's Irish Americans were professional or white-collar workers; nationwide the figure was only 6 percent. Irish Americans had surpassed blacks but still lagged behind all other European ethnic groups.

At the turn of the century the social position of Irish Americans began to improve, largely as the result of an event that had little to do with the group itself. The United States's emergence as a wealthy industrial power attracted new immigrant groups from other, less familiar corners of the map, including Italy, Russia, Austria-Hungary, Romania, and Serbia. In 1914, less than one sixth of America's immigrants came from what had once been the three main points of origin—Germany, Scandinavia, and the British Isles.

The shifting immigration pattern benefited Irish Americans, who came to be regarded as part of the native population. Their origins, after all, were in the British Isles, the point of departure for the nation's founders; they spoke English, they were usually fair skinned, and above all, they were familiar—especially compared to Italians, Jews, and eastern Europeans, with their alien languages, customs, and diets. In a nation growing in diversity, Irish immigrants and their children seemed homegrown.

Irish Americans were therefore exempted from the mounting animosity toward the new immigrants. Religion, once the great stumbling block for Irish Catholics, suddenly mattered less than race, as wildly distorted talk circulated about the need for preserving America's "Nordic purity" from the threat of "inferior" eastern and southern races. This sentiment ultimately led to calls for an

Because of their Anglo-Saxon origins, Irish immigrants were sometimes spared the suspicion aimed at newcomers from other countries.

official policy meant to stem the immigrant tide, and in 1924 the United States passed the National Origins Act, severely limiting immigration on a nation-by-nation basis.

By that time, however, the Irish had already stopped coming to America in significant numbers. In 1921, Ireland at last won its independence from Great Britain, and there were new opportunities in the homeland for those who stayed. Irish Americans began to look less to the arrival of new immigrants to bolster their identity; instead they asserted their Irishness by emphasizing those ancestral traits that best served their efforts to blend into the mainstream. Irish Americans, at last, began to reach the top of the social and economic ladder. The country itself had moved to the forefront of industrial nations, and Irish Americans reaped important rewards. ∾

The unorthodox campaign tactics of
Boston's mayor James Michael
Curley spanned half a century.

THE
PUBLIC
WORLD

Centuries of struggle in Ireland had imbued its people with patriotism, courage, and patience. These qualities, transplanted to American soil, prepared generations of Irish Americans for the rough-and-tumble of party politics.

The big-city political machines were the symbol of their success. In addition to providing community services, political machines offered careers— at least to men. An ambitious young politician might begin as a "ward heeler," getting out the vote on election day and handling the small difficulties with landlords or the police that often ensnared constituents. He might then progress to district or precinct leadership, with greater territory to manage and oversee. The next step was to win an elective post as a city alderman or councilman. Such a career often culminated with a seat in the state legislature.

In 1928 Alfred E. Smith ran for president on the Democratic ticket, but lost to Herbert Hoover.

Even those lacking the talent or temperament for politics often relied on political organizations to further their job prospects. Powerful machines were famous for "patronage," using their influence to gain control of government jobs. State and federal laws created jobs that were parceled out to the deserving (and sometimes the undeserving) by officeholders who themselves frequently had ties to Irish-American political organizations. The recipients of patronage jobs, and their families, repaid their debt at the polling station.

But personal favors were not enough on which to build a political base, and shrewd Irish-American politicians broadened their support by reaching beyond the narrow constituency of their own neighborhoods. Other large populations of have-nots—Italian and Jewish Americans, for example, as well as union members—were willing to back Irish-American politicians who could make good on their campaign promises. This Irish-American pragmatism sometimes took on a seamier aspect, especially at the local level, as it did in the case of Boston's mayor James Michael Curley.

Born in 1874, Curley entered Democratic party politics in an era when the political landscape was ruled by Republicans, mostly descended from old, established families often prejudiced against newcomers, especially Irish-Catholic immigrants and their offspring. A common sense of exclusion bound the outsiders, and Curley capitalized on their resentment, skillfully interweaving the resources of neighborhood organizations with the dictates of the Roman Catholic church.

By the turn of the century Curley had acquired a personal following in the neighborhoods by providing needed services and doling out patronage jobs. He was accused of corruption more than once and actually engineered election victories from behind bars, but few local politicians have ever attained the sweeping appeal Curley enjoyed. He remained a force in Boston politics until the 1950s.

Similar Irish-American city bosses of the same era included Charles F. Murphy of New York, Frank Hague of Jersey City, Thomas J. Pendergast of Kansas City, Edward J. Kelly of Chicago, and David L. Lawrence of Pittsburgh. The votes they controlled produced a flock of state and national leaders. Many came to prominence after the 1932 election of President Franklin D. Roosevelt—himself a protégé of New York's governor Alfred E. Smith, who in 1928 became the first Irish Catholic to win the Democratic nomination for president.

Roosevelt, who had dealt with Tammany Hall since his early days in the New York state legislature, included a number of Irish Americans in his 1932 administration, among them James A. Farley, chairman of the Democratic National Committee; Thomas G. Corcoran, a member of the "brain trust" that devised the New Deal, Roosevelt's innovative program for rescuing the nation from bankruptcy; and Frank Murphy, the governor of Michigan. In addition, a growing number of Irish-American senators and congressmen reflected the progress of this ethnic group in regional politics and, just as importantly, set the pattern for a future generation of elected officials.

As the 20th century wore on, the pragmatic approach of Irish-American reform politicians, who worked gradually for small gains rather than for wholesale changes in the overall system, came to dominate the thinking not only of the New Deal but also of Harry S. Truman's Fair Deal, the New

James Farley was chairman of the Democratic party in the 1930s.

Frontier of John F. Kennedy, and the Great Society of Lyndon B. Johnson.

The election of President John F. Kennedy in 1960 was the culmination of this process and a high point of Irish-American experience. Kennedy's grandfather P. J. Kennedy was a refugee from the Great Famine who immigrated to the United States in the mid-19th century and settled in Boston. His son, Joseph P. Kennedy, was a Harvard graduate who made a fortune in banking and in the stock market. Joseph Kennedy entered politics at the behest of Franklin D. Roosevelt, who appointed him chairman of the newly formed Securities and Exchange Commission, a watchdog agency that regulated Wall Street traders. He left politics in 1940 after a controversial term as U.S. ambassador to Great Britain.

Joseph Kennedy's greatest contribution to American politics issued from his marriage to Rose Fitzgerald, the daughter of Boston mayor John F. Fitzgerald, known as "Honey Fitz." The couple embodied the Irish-American dedication to family, and their children were raised as devout Catholics, intensely loyal to their clan and fiercely competitive when they entered the greater world.

John F. Kennedy, the second-oldest child of this remarkable family, was born in 1917. After graduating from Harvard, he enlisted in the navy and served in the Pacific as the commander of a

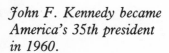

John F. Kennedy became America's 35th president in 1960.

torpedo boat during World War II. In 1946, he won a seat in the House of Representatives with the assistance of Boston's political machine.

Six years later he was elected senator from Massachusetts, and in 1960, at the age of 43, he became the youngest elected president in U.S. history. His very narrow victory over Richard M. Nixon was achieved with the aid of the Democratic party machine in Chicago, perhaps illegally—scholars are still divided. After less than three years in office, Kennedy's spectacular career turned tragic when he was assassinated in Dallas, Texas, on November 22, 1963.

Admired for his youthful good looks and his personal grace and charm, Kennedy was a hero not only to Irish Americans but also to the country at large, which saw in him a new kind of politician, equally at home at Harvard and in Hollywood. His presidency coincided with the emergence of the United States as the world's dominant power, and his confident manner summed up America's own self-image.

After his death, the "Kennedy mystique" steadily enveloped the entire family. John's younger brother Robert F. Kennedy served as U.S. attorney general and as a senator from New York, and was campaigning for the Democratic presidential nomination when he, too, was assassinated, on June 5, 1968. A third brother, Edward M. Kennedy, a Massachusetts senator, nearly captured the presidential nomination in 1980. Another generation of Kennedy politicians appeared in 1986, when Robert's son, Joseph Kennedy III, at the age of 33, was elected to the same congressional seat first held by John F. Kennedy nearly 40 years before.

In 1986 Robert Kennedy's son Joseph won the same congressional seat captured by his uncle John 40 years before.

Labor Leaders

George Meany became president of the powerful AFL-CIO when the two giant labor organizations merged in 1955.

Politics was not the only avenue available to Irish Americans reared on the values that the Kennedys embodied so glamorously. Irish Americans have distinguished themselves in other areas. The labor movement, for example, led by Irish immigrants in the 19th century, continued to attract Irish-American talent in the 20th.

Mike Quill and Joe Curran, both raised on the streets of New York's poor Irish community, emerged as important union organizers. In 1939, Curran became the first president of the National Maritime Union, which he himself established; and in the 1960s Quill founded the Transport Workers of America. Thereafter nearly all the top officials in both organizations bore Irish surnames. Another labor leader, George Meany, the grandson of a famine refugee, headed the American Federation of Labor, a powerful force in the nation's economy and politics.

Perhaps the most noteworthy of all Irish-American labor leaders was Terence Vincent Powderly (1849–1924). Born in Carbondale, Pennsylvania, to poor immigrant parents, Powderly became a railroad worker at the age of 13 and later became a machinist, a job he held for many years. In 1871 he joined the Machinists' and Blacksmiths' national union, and before long was its president.

Three years later Powderly joined the secret organization known as the Knights of Labor. Although bitterly opposed by owners and managers, the Knights soon developed into the largest and most influential force in the burgeoning American labor movement. Powderly rose to head the organization as "Grand Master Workman." He held this post from 1879 to 1893, a period during which he toured the nation to advance the cause for all workingmen.

Powderly's approach to labor issues was conciliatory. He rejected the concept of a class conflict pitting owner against workers and rejected the popular call for a new political party that would represent labor interests exclusively. Under Powderly's moderate stewardship, the Knights of Labor reached their peak of power in 1886, when membership totaled nearly 1 million.

Thereafter, as working conditions became more oppressive and industrial magnates strengthened their opposition, the organization faltered, along with the entire labor movement. Not until the turn of the century did the movement make new gains, with the emergence of the American Federation of Labor (AFL), led by Samuel Gompers, whose conciliatory outlook resembled Powderly's. No longer a dominant figure, Powderly, spent his last years working for the AFL in a variety of positions.

Irish-American Sportsmen

Another competitive area where Irish Americans particularly excelled was sports. In the early 20th century professional boxing was an outlet for poor boys growing up in the often dangerous Irish neighborhoods of major cities. Many Irish-American pugilists fought in clubs and gyms throughout the country until the 1960s, when blacks emerged to dominate the field.

One of the most famous of Irish-American prizefighters was John L. Sullivan (1858–1918). A product of Boston's teeming Irish-American community, Sullivan was the last of the great "bare-

Paddy Ryan, a bare-knuckles brawler, held the world heavyweight crown in the 1880s.

Two Irish-American baseball legends, managers John McGraw and Connie Mack, led rival teams into three World Series from 1905 to 1913.

knuckles" brawlers, though his career lasted into the era when boxers began to wear padded gloves. He became heavyweight champion in 1892 when he defeated Irish-born Paddy Ryan. A flamboyant personality who hated training, Sullivan captured the public imagination to such an extent that in 1887 the city of Boston presented him with a gold- and diamond-studded belt valued at $10,000, an exorbitant sum at the time. Five years later he lost his title to another Irish American, "Gentleman Jim" Corbett. The roster of exceptional Irish-American boxers also includes two later heavyweight champions, Jack Dempsey and Gene Tunney, who fought two historic title bouts in the 1920s.

A gentler sport, baseball, also had its share of Irish Americans who distinguished themselves as players, coaches, and managers. Cornelius McGillicuddy (better known as Connie Mack) was both owner and manager of the Philadelphia Athletics. His lean figure, clad in streetclothes, was a fixture in major league dugouts from the turn of the century until the 1950s, when, well into his eighties, he continued to act as field manager.

The Performing Arts

The abilities shared by public leaders and athletes include a gift for showmanship, for playing to the crowd and thriving in the glare of publicity. It is inevitable that Irish-American culture should also boast an impressive roster of professional stage and screen performers.

One of Broadway's leading stars was George M. Cohan (1878–1942) who wrote, directed, and scored dozens of musical comedies during the heyday of vaudeville, in the first two decades of the 20th century. His hit songs include "Yankee Doodle Dandy," "Give My Regards to Broadway," and, most famous of all, "Over There," the anthem sung by American troops headed to Europe to assist the Allies in World War I. Another Irish-American composer, Victor Herbert (1850–1924), created many of the country's best operettas, such as *Babes in Toyland* (1903), *The Red Mill* (1906), and *Eileen* (1917). Philip Barry (1896–1949) achieved prominence in the 1930s with his plays *Here Come the Clowns* (1938) and *The Philadelphia Story* (1939), later a successful film.

The greatest Irish American involved in the theater was also the first important American playwright, Eugene O'Neill (1888–1953). The son of an Irish-born matinee idol, who was also an alcoholic and a skinflint, the young O'Neill drifted in and out of occupations—as a prospector, sailor, reporter—and nearly died of tuberculosis before turning to drama. His early works, *The Emperor Jones* (1920), *The Hairy Ape* (1922), *Desire Under the Elms* (1924), and *Strange Interlude* (1928) were the first attempts to bring experimental theater to the American stage. They received lavish praise, as did *Mourning Becomes Electra*, a modernization of the ancient Greek tragedy, *The Oresteia*.

The recipient of several Pulitzer Prizes and the 1936 Nobel Prize for literature, O'Neill would nonetheless be merely a curiosity today had he not gone on to write his masterworks, *The Iceman Cometh* (1946), *A Moon for the Misbegotten* (1947), and, especially, *Long Day's Journey into Night* (1940), an autobiographical drama that covers one horrific 24-hour span in the life of the playwright, his older brother, and their parents. This portrait

George M. Cohan was one of vaudeville's brightest stars.

of a ruined family may be the greatest piece of theater ever written by an American, and it is so rooted in O'Neill's own experience that he hid it from the public until after his death.

By the 1920s the Broadway stage had lost much of its popularity to moving pictures, and Irish-Americans made a major impact on the screen.

The most distinguished of all Irish-American film actors and perhaps the preeminent actor of his generation was Spencer Tracy, whose long career spanned nearly four decades. Tracy began acting in college theater productions, then appeared in summer stock, eventually reaching the Broadway stage in the 1920s. When sound was introduced to feature movies in 1927, his expressive voice made him a natural for that medium, and in the 1930s he established himself as one of Hollywood's most versatile stars. He won consecutive Academy Awards for his portrayal of a fisherman in *Captains Courageous* (1937) and a priest in *Boys Town* (1938), both fine dramatic performances.

Eugene O'Neill (in the pinstripe suit) was the only American playwright ever awarded the Nobel Prize.

Tracy's real forte, however, was the subtler art of comedy; teamed with Katharine Hepburn in a succession of films, most notably *Woman of the Year* (1942) and *Adam's Rib* (1949), he played to perfection that most universal of male roles, the husband, his face a mobile mask of humorous wisdom, his voice effortlessly scaling a range of emotions. No one conveyed better the sense of being the lone sane presence in a world spinning toward madness; and in his best moments, such as the classic scene in *Woman of the Year* in which he struggles valiantly to remain calm during his bride's disastrous first attempt at preparing breakfast, Tracy's artistry is such that we forget we are watching a performance and feel instead that we are glimpsing an unguarded moment in the life of an actual man.

Tracy was not alone in helping to alert filmgoers to the virtues of the Irish character. The energy, wit, and toughness of James Cagney; the suave, relaxed crooning of Bing Crosby; the muscular acrobatics of Gene Kelly; and the delicate gentility of Maureen O'Sullivan and Grace Kelly reinforced traits that could be traced back to the beginnings of Celtic culture. ❧

Some critics consider Spencer Tracy the greatest film actor of his era.

*John Carroll became America's first
Catholic bishop in 1789.*

THE PRIVATE WORLD

Even as some Irish Americans have achieved prominence in the public realms of politics, labor, sports, and show business, others have added to the luster of our spiritual and intellectual life. As in Ireland, however, these different areas overlap. The leaders of Irish Catholicism, for instance, often carry their message beyond the pulpit. And the most imaginative Irish-American writers explore the wide variety of their country's social experience.

Religious Leaders

Irish immigrants were the first group to establish Catholicism as a major faith in America, so it is not surprising that Irish Americans rose to eminence as servants of the Roman Catholic church. The first American bishop was John Carroll (1735–1815), whose achievements unfolded against a backdrop of anti-Catholicism.

Born in Maryland, Carroll studied and taught in France. In 1774, when revolutionary fervor seized the colonies, Carroll returned home to take up the cause of independence. Two years later, he accompanied his friend Benjamin Franklin to Canada in an unsuccessful attempt to enlist Canadian support for the American rebels.

Although he was acquainted with the emergent country's leading political figures, Carroll met with great resistance in his effort to secure religious freedom and political equality for Catholics, who in many states were even denied the right to vote. In 1789, Carroll became Bishop of Baltimore, the leading center of Catholic activity in early American history. Vigorous and ambitious, Carroll soon established a Catholic college in Washington, D.C. (eventually it became known as Georgetown University), and he actively encouraged the church to set up missions for American Indians. Despite his efforts, discrimination against Roman Catholics remained commonplace in the United States long after Carroll's death.

A later figure, Archbishop Fulton J. Sheen (1895–1979), drew favorable attention to the Catholic church through his popular writings and his successful prime-time television program. Born in rural Illinois to Irish-American farmers, Sheen received a parochial education and entered the seminary in 1939. He earned graduate degrees from Catholic University in Washington, D.C., and from the University of Louvain in Belgium. His early career included a post in a poor parish in Peoria, Illinois, and a professorship of philosophy at Catholic University.

Sheen's eloquence attracted wide attention, particularly in New York City, where in the 1930s he preached regularly to overflow crowds. By 1950, his sermons, broadcast over a radio network of 118 stations, reached an audience estimated at 4 million. His many books explaining theology made that difficult subject accessible to general readers and lifted him on to the best-seller lists. The Archbishop's weekly television program, "Life Is Worth Living," first aired in 1951, achieved the top rating in its evening slot.

Even after he abandoned the airwaves, Sheen remained a major public figure for two decades, during which his views drifted toward controversial subjects. He advocated social welfare for the poor and also protested America's involvement in the Vietnam War. His most important achievement, however, was as a gifted communicator who raised the nationwide esteem of the Catholic church.

Irish-American Writers

Since the dawn of Celtic culture, Irish spiritual life was celebrated not only in the chapel but also through the workings of the free imagination. In antiquity, the Druids combined a feeling for divinity with a rich tradition of art and literature; like them, modern Irish authors have created a vibrant literature out of a combination of worldly knowledge and fabular invention.

In the United States this legacy reached fruition in the 20th century, when Irish Americans became leading proponents of "realism," a movement that used the novel and the short story to make a fictional record of ordinary, everyday life. Major Irish-American realists include James T. Farrell (1904–1979), author of the depression trilogy *Studs Lonigan* (1932–1935). Its doomed hero, wearing

Archbishop Fulton Sheen's sermons were broadcast on television in the 1950s.

Novelist and playwright John O'Hara was a leading practitioner of realism.

"the scar of immigration," falls victim to the narrow-minded and mean-spirited Chicago neighborhood where the author himself grew up. Farrell's reputation has dimmed since the 1930s, but he had a great influence on later novelists such as Norman Mailer and James Jones.

Another prominent realist was John O'Hara (1905–1970), the author of hundreds of short stories, mainly published in the *New Yorker*, and of novels, chiefly *Appointment in Samarra* (1934) and *Ten North Frederick* (National Book Award, 1955). Much of O'Hara's work is set in a fictionalized version of his hometown, Pottsville, Pennsylvania, which he dissects with minute and sometimes malicious precision, employing reportorial skills he honed as a newspaperman. At his best, in a dozen or so imperishable brief stories, O'Hara's fiction rises above the merely documentary and achieves a subtlety of expression and mood that rival the short fiction of such European masters as Maupassant and Turgenev.

Another great Irish-American writer, Flannery O'Connor (1925–1964), came from Milledgesville, Georgia, a small town in the Deep South. A devout Catholic, O'Connor transformed her native landscape into a grotesquely rendered wasteland of spiritual emptiness lit with bizarre humor and enriched with the grand religious themes of doubt, faith, and redemption. Her most famous stories, such as "A Good Man Is Hard to Find" and "Everything That Rises Must Converge," with their unfaltering narratives and uncanny psychological insight, helped shape contemporary American fiction. She died at 39 after a long, painful bout with lupus, a degenerative disease that forced her to spend her last years as an invalid.

The greatest Irish-American writer, F. Scott Fitzgerald (1896–1940), combined a talent for realism with a profound moral vision. Born in St. Paul, Minnesota, and later educated at Princeton (though he never earned his degree), Fitzgerald gained early fame with his first novel, *This Side of Paradise*, published when he was 23. In it and in short stories written at about the same time, Fitzgerald emerged as the spokesman of what he dubbed the "jazz age," a phrase still used to describe the American spree that followed World War I, when a young generation scandalized their elders with late-night parties, heavy drinking, and reckless driving.

After *The Beautiful and Damned* (1922), another hymn to "flaming youth," Fitzgerald ripened into an artist, and in 1925 published *The Great Gatsby*, an encapsulation of the Roaring Twenties and one of the half dozen legitimate claimants to the elusive

F. Scott Fitzgerald and his wife, Zelda, embodied 1920s glamour.

William Kennedy received the 1984 Pulitzer Prize for Ironweed.

title of "Great American Novel." Set against the glamorous background of luxurious Long Island estates, where hedonistic Ivy Leaguers consort with mobsters and showgirls, *Gatsby* dramatizes a central contradiction of our culture, that the beguiling hopefulness of the "American Dream" often coincides with a violent drive for material gain and a cynical lust for power.

Fitzgerald's other major work, *Tender Is the Night* (1934), depicts the dissolute life of wealthy Americans joy-riding through European capitals while their personal lives unravel. Though inferior to *Gatsby* in form and characterization, *Tender Is the Night* has much brilliant writing and provides many clues to the turmoil of Fitzgerald's own doomed life, a tragedy of imprudence that included alcoholism, a destructive marriage, and a disastrous screenwriting stint in Hollywood, where he repeatedly clashed with studio moguls who tampered with his work. He died in obscurity at the age of 44, halfway through a final novel, *The Last Tycoon*, whose posthumous publication revived a reputation that now ranks alongside that of his Nobel Prize-winning colleagues, William Faulkner and Ernest Hemingway.

Fitzgerald's Canadian contemporary, Morley Callaghan, also contributed to 20th-century fiction. Born in Toronto in 1903, Callaghan began publishing short stories while still in his early twenties. Soon he joined the North American artist community living in Paris, an experience recounted in his memoir, *That Summer in Paris* (1963). Although he never achieved the renown of his illustrious friends, Fitzgerald and Hemingway, Callaghan evolved into a deft craftsman with a spare yet evocative prose style, equally at home in short stories and the novel. *The Many-Colored Coat* (1960), a powerful tale enriched with biblical overtones, is set in Toronto, as is much of Callaghan's work.

No writer fuses the cultures of Ireland and North America more expertly than Brian Moore, who was born in Belfast in 1921, emigrated to Canada in 1948, and moved to the United States in 1959. A masterful storyteller whose conversational prose plumbs great psychological depths, Moore writes best about lonely failures who fall victim to their own delusions, as in *The Lonely Passion of Judith Hearne* (1956). *The Luck of Ginger Coffey* (1963), a bruising comedy about an Irish immigrant in Canada, captures all the hopefulness and disappointment of the immigrant experience. Moore has also written about his native Ulster, and its troubles, in *Catholics* (1972).

The Irish-American literary tradition flourishes today in the work of several writers, including

Mary McCarthy is one of America's preeminent women of letters.

Philip H. Sheridan helped guide Union forces to victory in the Civil War.

J. F. Powers (*Morte D'Urban*, a witty study of midwestern Catholicism), William Kennedy, and Mary Gordon. Kennedy's *Albany Trilogy*, which includes *Legs, Billy Phelan's Greatest Game*, and *Ironweed* (Pulitzer Prize, 1984), beautifully recreates an East Coast city during the depression, when Albany's downtown streets were a neon arcade of pool halls, bowling alleys, and all-night cafes. His nonfiction book, *O, Albany!*, features colorful portraits of the kingpins who manipulated that city's political machine.

Mary Gordon caused a sensation with her first novel, *Final Payments* (1978), the story of a young woman's struggle to shed the corset of her strict Catholic upbringing and to live guiltlessly as a modern woman, with an array of baffling choices open to her. A poet as well as a fiction writer, Gordon infuses lyrical intensity into traditional Catholic themes such as the high cost of obeying authority.

The outstanding living Irish-American writer is Mary McCarthy, who has published many works of fiction, memoirs, and essays. Born in Seattle, Washington, in 1912, she was raised by strict relatives in Minnesota, a cruel experience recounted in *Memories of a Catholic Girlhood* (1957) and *How I Grew* (1987). After graduating from Vassar College in 1933, she joined a circle of prominent New York intellectuals associated with *Partisan Review*, the leading literary magazine of the day. As its drama critic, McCarthy captured a following with her erudition, intellect, and razory wit. These qualities also illuminate such novels as *The Groves of Academe* (1954), a satire of university life, and *The Group*, a portrait of Vassar graduates and a bestseller in 1963. McCarthy writes more for the mind

The 1893 Chicago World's Fair featured the architectural wonders of Louis Sullivan.

than the emotions, and her forte is the literary essay. Deeply and widely educated, she easily handles a vast range of topics—opera, fiction, politics, and history.

The gallery of accomplished Irish Americans includes many other noteworthy figures. General Philip Henry Sheridan, for instance, was the Union army's finest cavalry officer during the Civil War. Louis H. Sullivan, the country's first world-class architect, was a pioneer of skyscraper design. *New York Daily News* journalist Jimmy Breslin won the Pulitzer Prize in 1986. James Tobin, a Yale professor, won the Nobel Prize for Economics in 1981. And a third-generation Irish American, Ronald Reagan, became our 40th president in 1980, and one of the most popular in history.

Perhaps the surest sign of the impact Irish Americans have made on our culture is the difficulty many of us have distinguishing them as an ethnic group; day by day, strains of the unique Irish-American character continue to filter into all our lives. ❧

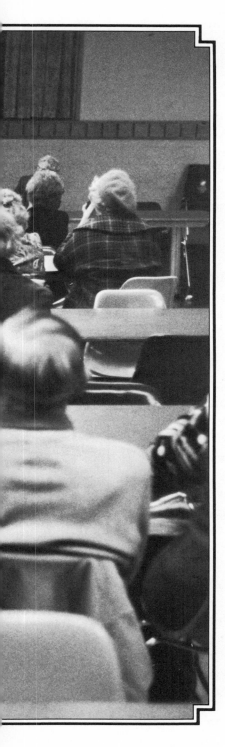

In 1987 citizens gathered in Woodlawn, New York, to discuss the problems posed by Irish illegal aliens.

SUMMING UP

The latest chapter in the Irish-American experience proves that immigration and assimilation are not mere stages in the history of ethnic groups but, rather, ongoing processes that change with time and circumstance.

Official records show that in 1986 fewer than 1,900 Irish were granted permanent residency in the United States, and that Irish-born Americans now form a minuscule percentage of the overall population, far less than 1 percent. Experts claim, however, that these numbers are meaningless because they fail to take into account a large underground population of Irish visitors who unlawfully overstay their allotted time in the United States.

Like other illegal aliens, those from Ireland try to elude immigration authorities by melting into the larger society, passing themselves off as citizens. The difference is that very few underground Irish are ever detected and sent home. In 1985, only 8 Irish were deported, compared with 11,368 Mexicans and 3,034 Salvadorans. Their success rests on two facts: Irish newcomers look and often sound like native Americans, and they shun the occupations (such as agriculture) that attract most other illegal aliens. In contemporary America, with its diverse ethnic palette, refugees from the British

Isles seem to hold an advantage over other arrivals, just as they did a century ago.

There are other ways in which the experience of Irish illegal aliens in the 1980s parallels that of their 19th-century precursors. The Great Famine, the crisis that drove so many early immigrants from their homeland, has a modern-day counterpart in Ireland's severe job shortage. From 1982 to 1987 Ireland's unemployment soared from 9 to 19 percent, a total of 30 percent for youth. Some Irish Americans mail airplane tickets to relatives in the old country hungry for work in the United States, just as in the 1850s generous Irish Americans bought postal orders that covered the cost of steerage for desperate immigrants. Adrian Flanelly, a New York City radio host who personally delivered 60,000 Irish applications to Washington, D.C., to meet the deadline for a special immigration lottery, seems an heir to the *Pilot*, the Boston newspaper that rallied Irish Americans around the cause of kinsmen trapped across the ocean by poverty, starvation, and disease.

Today's Irish illegal aliens are arriving at a crucial time in Irish-American history. Never has the group been more removed from its ancestral origins. Many Irish Americans have blended so smoothly into the mainstream that the community as a whole has been scrubbed clean of some distinctive cultural traits. Neighborhoods that for generations formed a vibrant core of our older cities (New York, Chicago, Boston, and Philadelphia) have lost inhabitants to the suburbs or the southwestern sunbelt. And the tightly meshed unit of the Irish-American family has steadily unraveled. Intermarriage with other groups, once unheard of, is now the norm; as of 1960, Irish Americans have

been more likely to marry outside the community than within. Even the Catholic church, the bulwark of Irish identity, has lost its hold on Irish-American youth.

Like today's Irish immigrants, their 19th-century forebears relied on others to bear the cost of the journey.

Perhaps these fraying bonds will be mended by new arrivals from the Old World. Indeed there is evidence that illegal aliens have already begun to revive the heritage sometimes ignored by more established Irish Americans. In New York City, for example, the "new" Irish often settle in old immigrant neighborhoods in Manhattan, the Bronx, and Queens, where church attendance is on the rise and local nightclubs draw customers eager to hear traditional Irish folk music.

This willingness to embrace the past bodes well for an ethnic group with so storied a history. Even without the stimulus of new arrivals, Irish Americans are still a long way from writing off their ancient identity. For many, the age-old "troubles" remain a sore point, as New Yorkers know from protests staged daily outside the British embassy by supporters of Ulster Catholics. And every March 17, when millions of Irish Americans pay nationwide tribute to St. Patrick, the Apostle of Ireland, other Americans take note of the huge population in their midst with a proud link to a tiny homeland across the ocean. ❧

FURTHER READING

Birmingham, Stephen. *Real Lace: America's Irish Rich.* New York: Harper and Row, 1973.

Breslin, Jimmy. *The World of Jimmy Breslin.* New York: Avon, 1976.

Farrell, James T. *Studs Lonigan.* New York: Avon, 1976.

Fitzgerald, F. Scott. *The Great Gatsby.* New York: Charles Scribner's Sons, 1925.

Griffin, William D. *Irish in America.* New York: Charles Scribner's Sons, 1981.

Joyce, James. *Dubliners.* New York: Penguin, 1976.

Kennedy, William. *O Albany! An Urban Tapestry.* New York: Viking Press, 1983.

Orel, Harold, ed. *Irish History and Culture: Aspects of a People's Heritage.* Lawrence: University Press of Kansas, 1976.

Riordan, William L. *Plunkitt of Tammany Hall.* New York: Alfred A. Knopf, 1948.

Shannon, William V. *The American Irish.* New York: The Macmillan Company, 1963.

Wakin, Edward. *Enter the Irish-American.* New York: Crowell, 1976.

INDEX

ACKNOWLEDGMENTS

Cover photo courtesy of the Library of Congress

We would like to thank the following sources for providing photographs: Angel Franco/The New York Times: p. 103; AP/Wide World Photos: p. 98; Art Resource: p. 50; The Bettmann Archive: pp. 14, 27, 29, 30, 40, 63, 65, 97, 99; The Bettmann Archive/BBC Hulton: p. 26; The Boston Public Library: p. 80; The British Library: p. 18; Brown Brothers: p. 31; Culver Pictures: pp. 17, 69, 79, 87, 88, 90, 96, 101; The Fotomas Index: p. 21; Gisele Freund/Photo Researchers: pp. 33, 52 (bottom); *Harper's Weekly:* pp. 45, 72, 73; *The Illustrated London News*: p. 60; Irish Tourist Board: pp. 49, 51, 52 (top); John F. Kennedy Library: p. 56; Library of Congress: pp. 12, 22, 24, 42, 44, 46, 53 (top), 64, 75, 76, 82, 105; Mario Suriani: Photoreporters: p. 54; Martha Swope: p. 53 (bottom); Museum of the City of New York: pp. 58, 67, 77, 89; National Archives: p. 100; National Portrait Gallery, Smithsonian Institution: p. 93; *New York Illustrated News*: p. 62; New York Public Library Picture Collection: pp. 36, 57; Seaman's Bank for Savings FSB: p. 39; Smithsonian Institution: pp. 43, 70; Union Pacific Railroad Museum Collection: p. 66; UPI/Bettmann Newsphotos: pp. 32, 55, 83, 84, 85, 86, 91, 95; Virginia State Library: p. 34. Photo Research: PAR/NYC.

J. F. WATTS, history professor and department chairman at the City College of New York, holds a Ph.D. from the University of Missouri. His publications include *Generations: Your Family in American History* as well as various essays on and reviews of social and diplomatic history. He has been a Younger Humanist Fellow of the National Endowment for the Humanities and has received the Outstanding Teacher Award from CCNY.

DANIEL PATRICK MOYNIHAN is the senior United States senator from New York. He is also the only person in American history to serve in the cabinets or subcabinets of four successive presidents—Kennedy, Johnson, Nixon, and Ford. Formerly a professor of government at Harvard University, he has written and edited many books, including *Beyond the Melting Pot, Ethnicity: Theory and Experience* (both with Nathan Glazer), *Loyalties,* and *Family and Nation.*